FOCUS ON EDUC

Series Editor: Tre

Teaching History

A teaching skills workbook

Jon Nichol M.A., Ph.D. Cantab
School of Education,
University of Exeter

Macmillan Education

© John Nichol 1984

All rights reserved. No reproduction, copy or transmission
of this publication may be made without written permission.

No paragraph of this publication may be reproduced, copied
or transmitted save with written permission or in accordance
with the provisions of the Copyright Act 1956 (as amended).

Any person who does any unauthorised act in relation to
this publication may be liable to criminal prosecution and
civil claims for damages.

First published 1984
Reprinted 1985

Published by
MACMILLAN EDUCATION LTD
Houndmills, Basingstoke, Hampshire RG21 2XS
and London
Companies and representatives
throughout the world

Printed in Hong Kong

British Library Cataloguing in Publication Data
Nichol, Jon
 Teaching history
 1. History—Study and teaching
 I. Title
 907'.1   LB1581
ISBN 0-333-36078-8

To Rosalind

ACKNOWLEDGEMENTS

The author and publishers wish to thank the following who have kindly given permission for the use of copyright material:

Basil Blackwell Publisher Ltd for an extract from *The Normans* by Jon Nichol; The Historical Association for the article 'How to evaluate a History Department' by John Higham in *Teaching History*, June 1979, and an extract from the pamphlet *Educational Objectives for the Study of History* by J.B. Coltham and J. Fines; Oxford University Press for an extract from *The Idea of History* by R.G. Collingwood; Schools Council for extracts from *Place, Time and Society 8-13: an Introduction* by Alan Blyth, Ray Derricott, Gordon Elliot, Hazel Sumner and Allan Waplington (1975); Maurice Temple Smith Ltd for an extract from 'History and the Social Sciences' by D. Heater, in *New Movements in the Study and Teaching of History* (1970).

CONTENTS

Editor's Preface   4
Introduction   5

PART 1 PREPARING TO TEACH HISTORY

Topic 1   Background reading   6
Topic 2   Why teach history?   7
Topic 3   Teaching for skills   9
Topic 4   Teaching for concepts   11
Topic 5   History teaching and the historian's evidence   14
Topic 6   History or integration?   18
Topic 7   Thinking in history   20
Topic 8   New ideas in history   23
Topic 9   School organisation   27
Topic 10   The history department   28
Topic 11   Problems of class management   29
Topic 12   Lesson observation   31
Topic 13   Ready, steady, go – quiz time!   32

PART 2 TEACHING HISTORY

Focus 1   A day in the life of a history teacher   33
Focus 2   Lesson planning   35
Focus 3   Management techniques and teaching skills   38
Focus 4   Discussion leadership skills   40
Focus 5   Teacher interaction with the pupils   42
Focus 6   Handling ideas and concepts   44
Focus 7   Questions in the classroom   46
Focus 8   Individual pupils at work   49
Focus 9   Teaching slow learners   51
Focus 10   Teaching quick learners   53
Focus 11   Group work   54

PART 3 REFLECTIONS ON EXPERIENCE

Topic A   History teaching and language across the curriculum   57
Topic B   Pupil assessment   60
Topic C   Innovations in history teaching   62
Topic D   Examination work   64
Topic E   How to evaluate a history department   65

Further reading   71

EDITOR'S PREFACE

The titles in this series are designed to examine basic teaching skills in their respective subject areas. Each title is laid out as a workbook so that the practitioner can utilise his or her own classroom as a basis for progressive professional self-development.

Impetus for the series came out of the DES-financed Teacher Education Project, which ran from 1976 to 1980 in the Universities of Nottingham, Leicester and Exeter. That project explored general teaching skills: class management, questioning, explaining, and the handling of mixed ability classes and exceptional pupils. A direct outcome from the work of the Teacher Education Project was a series of skills workbooks under the general title *Focus*, which was published by Macmillan during the years 1981 and 1982.

It is, perhaps, a measure of the success of the *Focus* series that I was approached by a number of colleagues in the involved universities with the proposal for a 'curriculum' series of workbooks which would apply some of the teaching skills highlighted and researched by the project to specific subject areas.

Each title in the current curriculum series is aimed at subject teachers in the appropriate field. Our corporate intention is to make each workbook immediately relevant to the needs of three main groups of users: qualified teachers of the subject in question; teachers qualified in some other discipline who find themselves pressed into service on less familiar ground; and students in training in the subject area concerned. Past experience has led us to believe that each exercise is adaptable for use at various levels of sophistication according to the stage reached by the user and to his or her own needs.

Each workbook has a tripartite format. Part 1 is intended to start the user thinking about issues in the particular curriculum area, and the activities designed for this purpose can often be carried out away from the classroom itself. In Part 2 a collection of practical exercises encourages teachers to become more self-aware and to scrutinise their own practice. Part 3 helps the teachers reflect on practice and experience by relating classroom events to research and theory. Within this basic structure individual authors are given some flexibility to interpret their own theme.

The series makes frequent demands on teachers to get together in order to watch one another at work: a process we have labelled 'observational pairing'. Traditionally the classroom has been 'a fine and private place' as Marvell might have put it. We believe that professional self-respect demands that a more open attitude should prevail.

It is especially opportune to be producing the curriculum series of workbooks at a time when economic stringencies are making in-roads into the education service in general and into in-service provision in particular. There is mounting public pressure for increased accountability by the teaching profession. This series will, we believe, help to make teachers more analytical in their teaching and more articulate in expressing the rationale for their work. It will also fill a void for really practical advice for all those whose jobs involve a responsibility for professional training, as university and college tutors, inspectors, advisers, teachers' centre wardens and headteachers, and heads of subject departments.

Dr Trevor Kerry
University of Nottingham

INTRODUCTION

The origins of this book lie on the shelves of Professor E.C. Wragg's study at Exeter University. In 1979, when I arrived at Exeter as the tutor for the PGCE and M.Ed History courses, I visited Ted Wragg and was fascinated to see pilot copies of the Teacher Education Project *Focus* series on teaching skills. A surreptitious read through them was a revelation, and it struck me that many of their ideas could be adapted for use with initial trainees for history teaching. A quick chat with Ted led to the loan of a number of volumes, and the piecing together of an observation programme for our PGCE students. The success of the initial observation schedules led to the emergence of a booklet along the lines of others in the curriculum series.

The nature of this book is heavily dependent upon the 'onlie begetter', the Teacher Education Project. Many of the exercises contained in it are based on those carefully worked out for an examination of teaching skills, but the tasks have all been modified for use in the history classroom. During the past two years the scope of the work has changed radically. As well as it being an aid to initial main course history trainees, it is also aimed at those teaching history as a second subject, as an element in integrated or social studies or as part of the junior school curriculum. The focus of the work shifted, largely as a response to the interest teachers showed in the original draft of the book. Clearly it had far wider application than for initial trainees. It can be seen as a way into history teaching for the non-specialist, and has been written in response to market forces.

This book aims to make you a better teacher of history. It is not a magic wand that will solve all your problems, but we hope it will point to ways in which your teaching can improve. The booklet is in three parts: activities you can engage in away from the classroom as a preparation, during a period of teaching, and afterwards. The programme is accretionist, and aims to develop teaching confidence and improve classroom performance. Like the Holy Trinity, we hope that the tripartite nature of the course means that the whole will be greater than the sum of its parts.

Adapt the ideas and activities in this booklet to your individual circumstances. It is designed for individual study and use, as a way into history teaching which we hope is effective yet painless. The book does not intend to be a definitive statement of how history should be taught, nor an exhaustive and exhausting list of all the skills which a fully competent professional teacher will require. It is, rather, a map of an area of teaching practice, and we hope that you will find it a useful guide to what you encounter on the ground.

ACKNOWLEDGEMENTS

I would like to thank Ted Wragg for originally suggesting the writing of the history volume in the curriculum series, and him and Trevor Kerry for their encouragement and support during its gestation. Also, I would like to express my appreciation of students and teachers for their positive criticisms and suggestions. My greatest debt is to my past and present pupils, who still bring me weekly face-to-face with the realities of classroom teaching. Many of the activities suggested are borne out of my present teaching experiences, and are designed to try to remedy the only too obvious weaknesses and failings. If this book is of value to both trainees and experienced teachers in heightening awareness and sharpening skills, it will have been successful.

Part 1 PREPARING TO TEACH HISTORY

**Topic 1
BACKGROUND
READING**

This Topic aims to provide an introduction to some of the most relevant background reading and information relating to the teaching of history. Such reading should provide a firm foundation for your teaching in both theory and practice. Background reading also produces ideas and suggestions you might like to follow up.

**Activity 1:
Background reading**

Ask your school, college, university or department library to obtain these books and pamphlets if they do not already have them. Read the descriptions under each title, and work out the order in which you would like to consult the books and pamphlets.

Blyth, A. et al., 1976, *Place, Time and Society 8-13: Curriculum Planning in History, Geography and Social Science*, Collins. (A fascinating analysis of the application of the concepts-based approach to the teaching of integrated studies. Written as a handbook for teachers wishing to produce their own courses.)

Blyth, J.E., 1982, *History in Primary Schools*, McGraw-Hill. (A practical approach for teachers of 5-11-year-old children.)

Coltham, J.B. and Fines, J., 1971, *Educational Objectives for the Study of History*, Historical Association, TH35. (An attempt to apply the skills and objectives approach to the teaching of history. It has had a profound impact on teaching and examining.)

Dickinson, A.K. and Lee, P.J. (eds), 1978, *History Teaching and Historical Understanding*, Heinemann. (Contains chapters on evidence in the classroom, the objectives approach, language in history teaching and children's historical thinking.)

Levine, N., 1981, *Language Teaching and Learning – History*, Ward Lock. (A wide-ranging examination of language in history teaching.)

Nichol, J., 1980, *Simulation in History Teaching*, Historical Association, TH45. (An explanation of the use of games and simulations, illustrated with numerous examples from classroom use.)

Palmer, M. and Batho, G., 1981, *The Source Method in History Teaching*, Historical Association, TH48. (A practical introduction to the preparation and use of sources in the classroom.)

Rogers, P.J., 1971, *The New History: theory into practice*, Historical Association, TH44. (An examination of the philosophical basis for teaching history, related to practical examples.)

Steele, I., 1976, *Developments in History Teaching*, Open Books. (A clear introduction to the ideas underlying current history teaching. A range of chapters on new approaches in the classroom are most stimulating.)

Unwin, R., 1981, *The Visual Dimension in the Study and Teaching of History*, Historical Association, TH49. (An excellent analysis of the use of visual evidence for history teaching, with numerous practical suggestions.)

A subscription to the journal *Teaching History*, published three times yearly by the Historical Association, is well worth while. *Teaching History* contains numerous articles covering all facets of history teaching.

When you have put the list of titles into your own order of interest, read the first three (if you managed to obtain these three). Make brief notes as you go along. These can be the first contribution to a file of information and ideas you can build up throughout your period of study.

Activity 2:
Getting the reading habit

Continue reading throughout your period of study, and link this reading to the topics covered.

Topic 2
WHY TEACH HISTORY?

Ask a colleague or any member of your group, 'What is the point of learning maths at school?' It is likely that you will receive several good reasons. Try the same approach for history — and see if his or her ideas match your own. If you put the same question about history to a stranger in the street, you might end up with few if any reasons you would accept, and even suggestions about acceptable alternative forms of employment for history teachers!

Not all history teachers can articulate WHY they teach what they teach. From the start it is a good idea to sort out some ideas on this issue. The following Activity aims to help you and your discussion group (if you are a member of one) to reach some conclusions.

Activity 3:
Why teach history?

3.1 With a colleague, write down separately three answers to the question, 'What is the point of learning maths in school?' Discuss your own and your partner's list with him or her, and why they differ.

3.2 Below is a list of fifteen reasons for teaching history — the good, the bad and the ugly. Put the points into your order of preference. With your partner discuss the first five on both of your lists, and why they differ. Do the same for the bottom five. Then add any other reasons you can think of for teaching history.

1. The study of history is an essential part of our cultural heritage.
2. History develops a wide range of educational skills — such as comprehension, analysis, synthesis and extrapolation.
3. The historian deals with important ideas and concepts which every child should understand — ideas such as change, continuity, cause and consequences: and concepts like Marxism, Revolution and Imperialism.
4. History contains great literature.
5. History is a vital element in education for world citizenship.
6. History contributes to the school ethos.
7. History helps you understand your locality's development.
8. History provides jobs for unemployable history students and graduates.
9. History is a valid discipline — a unique process of enquiry which every child should experience.
10. History helps pupils come to terms with life.
11. History develops the acquisition and use of language.
12. History fosters empathy — the ability to understand how other people think and feel, and their positions and roles in society.
13. History makes pupils into good citizens and loyal supporters of the nation.
14. History is a valuable leisure activity.
15. History welds society together.

This Activity is difficult. Some of the reasons given above are open to a range of interpretations. Others fail to distinguish between different uses of the word history. Some begged questions, e.g. in a multicultural society, whose cultural heritage is being communicated? Some raise much wider questions, such as the language policy of schools.

One point not raised is how history is actually used. In our everyday lives history is constantly being used in many ways. Activity 3.3 aims to illustrate this, and provides an opportunity for reading newspapers in seminars.

3.3 Bring with you two or three newspapers from a single day. Read them through, and note which articles have any reference to historical events, or require some knowledge of history to understand them. Then try to classify the articles under headings worked out from the list above. This exercise should give you some idea of *how history is used* in our modern society.

3.4 When you have completed Activities 3.1, 3.2 and 3.3 you should be able to think of five good reasons for teaching history. Write each down as a clear statement. Then spend a paragraph justifying each reason you give. Lay out your work as below:

1   REASON:

   Justification:

2   REASON:

   Justification:

3   REASON:

   Justification:

4   REASON:

   Justification:

5   REASON:

   Justification:

Follow-up
1   For a sophisticated rationale for studying history, read Marwick, A., 1970, *The Meaning of History*, Macmillan.
2   In your reading of newspapers, magazines, *TV Times* and *Radio Times*, and your listening to radio and watching TV, think about how history is being used. Collect good and interesting examples, and add them to your course file.

Topic 3
TEACHING FOR SKILLS

In the 1960s history teachers were worried about the survival of their subject in schools. A twin threat arose from the emergence of integrated studies and the new social sciences, spearheaded by sociology. It was feared that history would be seen as an irrelevant subject on the curriculum, and be confined to the timetable junk room along with ballroom dancing and classics. Defenders of history in schools needed a sharper analytical weapon than had previously existed, and in 1971 J.B. Coltham and J. Fines provided it in their pamphlet, *Educational Objectives for the Study of History*. Coltham and Fines argued that it was possible to analyse the nature of historical study as a separate discipline, and then to categorise the skills which were needed to engage in that discipline. Such skills could be arranged in an order of progression which pupils could master. By exercising his or her skills upon historical evidence the student would be involved in the historical process. Such work would relate closely to the imaginative reconstruction of past historical situations. The Coltham and Fines pamphlet dovetailed neatly into ideas about resource-based and child-centred learning. The extracts below give an indication of the main thrust of the pamphlet.

What is an Educational Objective?

An 'educational objective', then, describes firstly what a learner can do as a result of having learned; and secondly, it describes what an observer (usually the teacher but it could be any interested person) can see the learner doing so that he can judge whether or not the objective has been successfully reached. And thirdly, the objective, in describing what the learner will have achieved, also indicates what educational experience he requires if he is to achieve the objective.

The Framework of the Pamphlet

Section A	Attitudes (of pupils) towards the study of history	Pages 6-9
	1 Attending	6
	2 Responding	7
	3 Imagining	7
Section B	Nature of the discipline	9-16
	1 Nature of information	10
	2 Organising procedures	12
	3 Products	13
Section C	Skills and abilities	16-23
	1 Vocabulary acquisition	16
	2 Reference skills	17
	3 Memorisation	18
	4 Comprehension	18
	5 Translation	18
	6 Analysis	19
	7 Extrapolation	20
	8 Synthesis	20
	9 Judgment and evaluation	21
	10 Communication skills	21
Section D	Educational outcomes of study	23-28
	1 Insight	25
	2 Knowledge of values	25
	3 Reasoned judgment	26

Section A is concerned principally with the *affective* aspects of the learners' personalities: the exercise of the feeling and willing behaviours. Without the emotional involvement indicated in this section, the study of a subject — any subject — cannot really be said to have begun; and without such involvement, the study cannot fruitfully continue... Feeling and willing cannot be exercised in a vacuum, and Section B gives an analysis of the particular *form of knowledge*, history, towards which these affective behaviours are to be directed. Section C sets out the *skills and abilities* relevant to the kind of knowledge described in Section B. Sections B and C are thus primarily concerned with cognitive behaviours. In the last section, D, there is a return to the affective area when outcomes of the study and practice of history are described in terms of their contribution to the *personal development* of the learner, both cognitive and affective.

The Historical Imagination

Imagining Since the material of history consists principally of human beings' activities in the past, study of this area of knowledge demands conative effort on the part of the learner to enter into, as it were, 'the shoes' or 'the skins' of people met only through such evidence as a description or a portrait... While 'imagination' at its simplest requires the formation of an image in the mind — and this may be pictorial or verbal; historical imagination requires not only this but usually something more: the words 'sympathy' and 'empathy' are useful here. Sympathy can be defined as 'the power of entering into another's feeling or mind', and empathy as 'the power of entering into another personality' and 'imaginatively experiencing his experience.' If a study of humans and their many activities is to demand something more than external acquaintance, sympathetic and empathetic behaviours are necessary.

Although the Coltham and Fines pamphlet has recently come under attack (see Follow-up) it has made history teachers consider in detail the aims and objectives of their history courses, and the skills which they develop. Significantly, *Educational objectives for the study of history* has affected the syllabuses drawn up by the Examination Boards, and the agreed *National Criteria for History and the 16+*. As such, it directly affects the kind of history taught to examination forms in the 14-16 age range.

Activity 4: Objectives in history teaching

1 Obtain the history syllabus of the school in which you work or to which you are attached. To what extent is the Coltham and Fines checklist of aims and objectives reflected in the syllabus?

2 Select a portion of the syllabus for the school in which you are working. Draw up a revised version, incorporating the ideas of Coltham and Fines.

3 Produce a scheme of work for the first term in which pupils are taught history, specifying the aims and objectives to be achieved during that period.

Follow-up

Discuss the value of Coltham and Fines' work for history teachers in the light of:

Gard, A. and Lee, P.J., 1978. ' "Educational Objectives for the Study of History" Reconsidered' in Dickinson, A.K. and Lee, P.J. (eds), *History Teaching and Historical Understanding*, Heinemann.

Fines, J., 1981, 'Educational Objectives for History ten years on', *Teaching History*, No. 30.

**Topic 4
TEACHING FOR
CONCEPTS**

Should we teach pupils *content*, a body of knowledge, or should our courses aim to develop an understanding of *concepts*? This could well be a false dichotomy, with both elements being essential for the development of understanding. However, implicit in many courses is a philosophical position based upon one of these two stances — content- or concept-based teaching.

The Schools Council *Place, Time and Society 8-13* project based its approach to humanities teaching upon the notion of teaching for conceptual understanding. It regarded the subject areas as *resources* upon which teachers and pupils could draw to develop a more general understanding of human development. This it illustrated in the form of a diagram:

> *The social disciplines of*
> History, Geography, Economics, Sociology,
> Social Anthropology, Social Psychology and
> Political Science

are resources available for the teaching of

> *the*
> *social subjects*
>
> *either*
>
> separately: or together:
> history, geography,   social studies,
> separate social   environmental studies,
> sciences   humanities, integrated
>   studies

in the study of

> *Man in Place, Time and Society*

In developing conceptual understanding the pupil would employ a range of intellectual and physical skills. These would relate to the development of personal qualities.

	SKILLS		PERSONAL QUALITIES
Intellectual	*Social*	*Physical*	*Interests, Attitudes, Values*
1 The ability to find information from a variety of sources, in a variety of ways. 2 The ability to communicate findings through an appropriate medium. 3 The ability to interpret pictures, charts, graphs, maps, etc. 4 The ability to evaluate information. 5 The ability to organise information through concepts and generalisations. 6 The ability to formulate and test hypotheses and generalisations.	1 The ability to participate within small groups. 2 An awareness of significant groups within the community and the wider society. 3 A developing understanding of how individuals relate to such groups. 4 A willingness to consider participating constructively in the activities associated with these groups. 5 The ability to exercise empathy (i.e. the capacity to imagine accurately what it might be like to be someone else).	1 The ability to manipulate equipment. 2 The ability to manipulate equipment to find and communicate information. 3 The ability to explore the expressive powers of the human body to communicate ideas and feelings. 4 The ability to plan and execute expressive activities to communicate ideas and feelings.	1 The fostering of curiosity through the encouragement of questions. 2 The fostering of a wariness of overcommitment to one framework of explanation and the possible distortion of facts and the omission of evidence. 3 The fostering of a willingness to explore personal attitudes and values and to relate these to other people's. 4 The encouraging of an openness to the possibility of change in attitudes and values. 5 The encouragement of worthwhile and developing interests in human affairs.

By exercising their intellectual, social and physical skills, related to their personal qualities, pupils would steadily increase their *conceptual* grasp.

What form did *conceptual* understanding take? The project identified seven key concepts for organising our understanding. Related to these key concepts were subsidiary concepts, which enable us to make sense of our environment. The study of Sheffield and the Peak District was a typical case.

Key Concept	*Peak District*	*Sheffield*
Communication	Routeways; materials; access to leisure pursuits.	Routeways; regional centre; multicultural contact.
Power	Prehistoric forts; Duke of Devonshire; dependence on outside decision making.	Expoitation of coal, coke and steel; social and political power.
Values and Beliefs	Survival of earlier value-systems; value of leisure pursuits.	Emergence of the social values of a modern city
Conflict/Consensus	Conflict over the use of open country, and transport routes; consensus over local autonomy.	Conflict of interests in the main industries and occupations and local groups; degree of civic consensus.
Similarity/Difference	Limestone and gritstone country; similarity of institutions.	City and suburb; heavy industry and light industry; employer and employed; similarity of local patriotism.

Key Concept	Peak District	Sheffield
Continuity/Change	Continuity in hill farming; change in economic use (extraction, water supply) and in role as 'lung' for three cities.	Transformation from a rural area to a Victorian industrial city and again to a modern regional centre; continuity in buildings and institutions.
Causes and Consequences	Individual instances, related to a complex system (a rural area may appear deceptively simple).	A clearly inter-related complex: (a city looks as complex as it is).

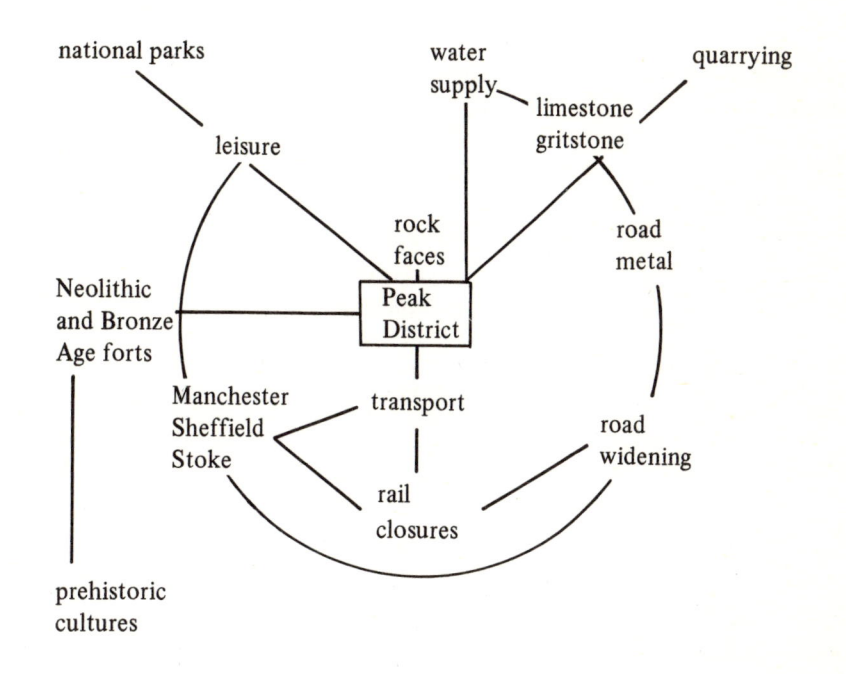

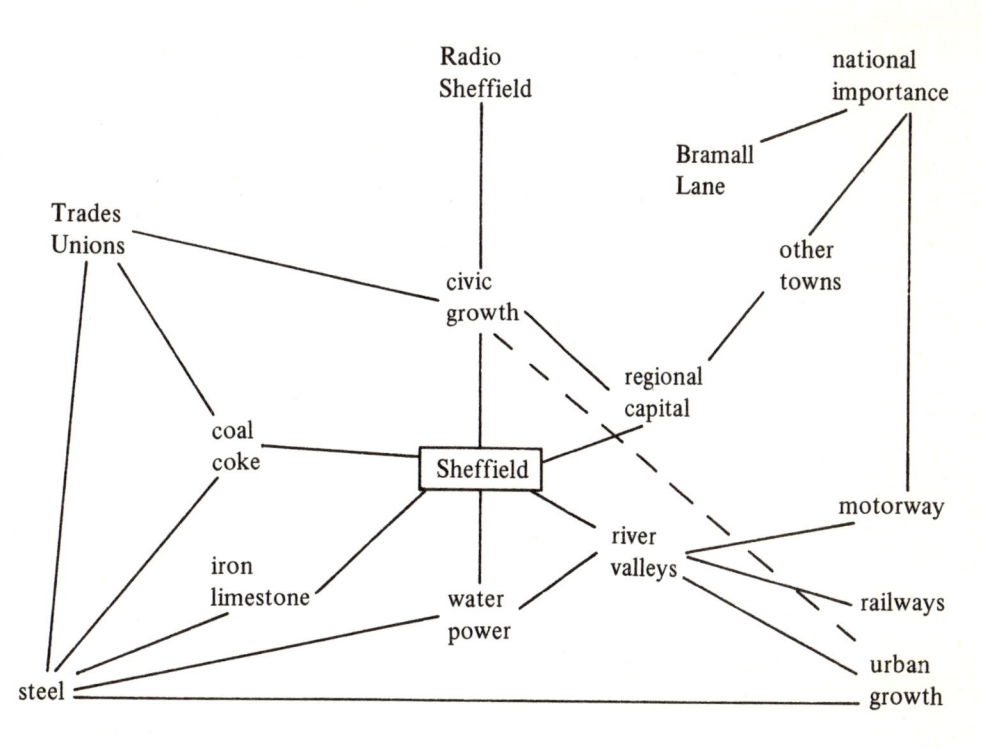

Such a concepts-based approach could be developed for your own school. A concepts-related course allows us to implement Jerome Bruner's 'spiral curriculum': at each stage of pupil education we return to the same concepts at an increasingly sophisticated level of understanding. This is based on the axiom that all subjects can be taught in an intellectually honest way from the start of a course of instruction. Learning can be visualised as a spiral staircase. During a course pupils would deepen their understanding of both key and subsidiary concepts.

In history teaching we can identify three types of concepts: structural, organisational and specific. Structural concepts are fundamental to the discipline as a whole, organisational are common to different periods, while specific concepts are terms which relate to a specific era. Focus 6 takes these ideas further.

Activity 5: Looking at historical concepts

1 Try to analyse your school's humanities or history teaching, using the concepts supplied by the *Place, Time and Society 8-13* project.

2 How useful are these concepts? What gaps do they suggest need to be filled in your school's lower school teaching?

Follow-up

1 Read Blyth, A. et al., 1976, *Place, Time and Society 8-13: Curriculum Planning in History, Geography and Social Science*, Collins, ESL. Using the ideas in the book, plan out a humanities curriculum for your own school or for a year-group you are currently teaching.

2 Read Bruner, J.S., 1960, *The Process of Education,* Knopf Vintage Books; and Bruner, J.S., 1966, *Towards a Theory of Instruction*, Belknap/Harvard. (These are perhaps the two most important books on education produced during the past twenty-five years. They also have the merit of being relatively short.)

**Topic 5
HISTORY TEACHING AND THE HISTORIAN'S EVIDENCE**

Teaching for skills and concepts are only two facets of current thinking about history teaching. Behind every history teacher's practice there should be a clear understanding of the nature of the knowledge which he or she is trying to get the pupils to learn. An academic discipline consists of three intermeshed kinds of knowledge: propositional (*know that*), procedural (*know how*) and conceptual (*organisational*). For history, propositional (*know that*) knowledge is the body of information that historians produce on a topic — their finished products. In schools it is the kind of information that is enshrined in countless textbooks, and is handed to the pupils as a received body of knowledge, the 'facts' of history. Procedural (*know how*) knowledge is how historians reach their conclusions — the process of enquiry that results in *know that*. *Know how* knowledge is concerned with the whole range of *activities* by which historians find out about the past. Conceptual knowledge involves the concepts which historians use to organise both their *know how* and *know that* knowledge.

The implications for the classroom are clear. The teacher should be as concerned with the process of enquiry as with the imparting of received knowledge. This leads to an active, child-centred form of learning in which the teacher plays a leading role. For the pupils to be involved in the learning process, they need to handle historical resources. The article below suggests what this means for the classroom teacher.

HISTORY TEACHING, THE HISTORIAN'S EVIDENCE AND PUPILS' HISTORICAL UNDERSTANDING

Publishers are now spawning a plethora of materials which claim to present historical 'evidence' in a palatable form for pupils in the 8-18 age range. As an author with a relatively fertile pen in this area, it might not come amiss to state some of the assumptions which led in my case to the marriage between the research and classroom historians. A number of beliefs are implicit in such unions whose children are resource-based history courses. The fathers or mothers of 'evidence'-based history teaching schemes consider that their classroom offspring either:

1. teach the pupils to understand what historians do, *or*
2. get pupils to simulate part or all of what the historian does, *or*
3. treat pupils as proto-historians, who carry out their own independent historical work as historians.

Clearly these approaches overlap. They can even represent a hierarchy of learning up which the pupil progresses, until he perches as the fully fledged historian upon the uppermost rung of the educational ladder. This model of pupils' historical progress is based upon the belief that historical study involves a process of enquiry and not merely the mastering of a received body of knowledge. Implicitly the historical process has an identifiable structure. Working with 'evidence' enables the pupil to achieve understanding and relative mastery of the historian's craft by the end of his education. If this is so, we must be able to relate history teaching to the work of the professional historian. In turn he should be able to recognise the links between his academic activities and pupils' historical work.

How can the 'evidence'-based approach to history teaching be reconciled with academic historical studies? Three linked ideas help us accept that pupils can participate in the historical process.

1. There is a pattern of historical study which they can engage in.
2. 'Evidence' in the classroom appears in an *edited* form. This editing means that an original historical source has been changed into an educational *resource*.
3. The pupil's attainment of historical understanding is a joint process which involves the pupil and his teacher. Together this *co-operative learning* involves a full range of the historian's activities.

The rest of this paper deals with these three ideas. Is there an acceptable pattern of historical study which pupil work can conform to? Philosophers of history have spent much energy on how professional historians work. Like scavenging ants the philosophers have poured over the corpus of historians' writings on their craft, and pointed out differences, nuances of interpretation and apparent contradictions between different authors. If we accept that each historian works in his own unique way, we can happily accept the inconsistencies which worry the philosophers. Most historians seem to share certain common ground:

1. Any historical writing must relate to a publicly accessible body of knowledge which academic historians have built up. Such knowledge is part of an ongoing historical debate which assimilates new ideas and hypotheses and factual information.
2. The historian brings to his work his 'second record', that is, his range of intellectual skills, his experience of life and his general historical understanding. His 'second record' provides him with the mental equipment with which to handle the historical 'first record' — the sources of history: the evidence which the past has left behind.
3. At some point in his reading upon an historical topic the historian begins to frame questions. As the evidence and the historian's ideas become increasingly sophisticated, new questions are formulated and old ones either resolved, modified or discarded.
4. The framing and answering of questions involves an enquiry into the nature and validity of the sources being used — both primary and secondary.
5. The historian recreates in his mind the historical situation or situations under review. This recreation allows him to answer the final set of questions he has upon the topic.
6. The historian is eclectic in the range of ideas and concepts he uses in his work. Many

are drawn from the modern world, and other social science disciplines. Underlying his work are some fundamental concepts — cause, change, continuity and consequence.

To be involved in this process of historical study the pupil must actively handle historical 'evidence'. Below we will only look at one element of primary sources — written evidence. To work on written sources the pupil must be able to understand them. For the sources to be accessible to all secondary pupils, there are four different levels at which they can handle written evidence. Each level is tied to the pupil's linguistic ability and his capacity for historical understanding. Palpably most written and manuscript sources are unintelligible in their original form to most pupils. Thus it is a nonsense to talk of them working on such sources from the start of their secondary schooling. At *the first level* of pupil involvement with historical sources they are heavily modified so that they are accessible to the majority of that particular year-group. Before the pupils can use them, most original sources need packaging and editing so that they are in a manageable form. The nature and amount of editing will depend upon the original's form and the audience for which it is intended. The turning of *sources* into *resources* for classroom use often entails a radical revision. The first step is to transcribe the original into a readable handwritten or typed script. Virtually all sources before 1700 AD demand this treatment. The process is even more elementary where the source has to be translated into modern English, either from medieval English or a foreign language. The second step is to modify any elements which can cause confusion — such as syntax, grammar, abbreviations and punctuation. Sir Lewis Namier followed this system in transcribing his source material for publication. The third element is to modify any archaisms and difficult vocabulary which will be beyond the grasp of the class. In this the teacher translates the original source into a form suitable for pupil use — that is, into children's English. A crucial factor is to match the source to the audience's reading age. The final element is to present the resource in an attractive and easy to handle form. The Schools Council History 13-16 Project's *Looking at evidence* (Holmes McDougall, 1976) shows the process at work of modifying *sources* and turning them into an edited classroom *resource*. On page 17, in the section dealing with knighthood, it prints:

'*Source 4 An Indenture* (a written agreement) made between the Earl of Warwick and Sir John Trafford in 1461. (Summary in modern English.) This agreement was made on 26th May in the first year of King Edward IV's reign between Richard Neville, Earl of Warwick, and Sir John Trafford . . .'

Above source 4 is a photograph of the original deed. My transcription of the original reads:

'This indenture made ye xxvi day of May the fyrst yere of ye Regne of the king our qondam lord Edward ye IV between Richard Neville erle of Warwyk, capitain of Caleye of ye one pte and Sr John Trafford knyght of the or pte.'

Selection of the kind of source material is equally important, particularly at level one. The source must be understandable at the pupil's stage of intellectual development. For many children its content has to be at the iconic (Bruner), or concrete operational stage (Piaget). Selectivity will also involve the omission of confusing or irrelevant passages — material which would hinder the pupil's understanding of the historical situation which the source material aims to bring to life.

At *the second level* the source is transcribed or translated from the original with the minimum modification. The major change occurs in removing it from its archival context, and in the omission of passages considered irrelevant. Such transcriptions often modify archaic spelling and grammar, and present the source in modernised English. The process is similar to level one, with the major difference of avoiding transliteration. Much of the resource material available in kit, booklet or book form is presented in this way. Such sources usually give a full contextual reference.

The third level involves the use of xerox copies or facsimiles of original sources. The key factor is their removal from their archival context. Evidence presented at this level requires an ability to transcribe and translate into modern English. Such unedited sources derive their resource nature from the way in which they are packaged and presented to the pupil.

At *the final level* the pupil handles the source in its archival context — whether it is a printed or manuscript piece of evidence. Using sources in context adds a different dimension to historical understanding. They allow source evaluation against the background of the original archive — an element missing in the presentation of evidence in levels one to three. Pupils working at level four need most of the professional historian's skills — the ability to decipher and interpret the source's meaning; to place it in its archival context; to see its relevance against the general understanding developed of the topic; and to use it as evidence to help answer the questions he has about the subject. The AEB pilot 'A' level history scheme has shown that many pupils can successfully handle sources at level four.

The final element in using 'evidence' in the classroom is *co-operative learning*. It involves the teacher and pupil in the *joint* development of historical understanding. Indeed, co-operative learning continues to the end of the historian's training. An integral element in the work of a Ph.D student is the role of his supervisor. At school the teacher provides the context for the resource material to make sense, and exercises and suggestions which enable the pupil to develop a rounded understanding of an historical situation. As the pupil develops the skill of the historian the teacher progressively plays a diminishing part in his learning. By the end of 'A' level the most able students are capable of functioning in relative independence when working on certain limited topics.

In the use of an historical *resource* or *resources* at levels 1-3 the teacher plays a crucial role in providing a framework of historical information, or access to it in the form of textbooks. A contextual framework is essential for making sense of resource material. The sophistication of the historical outline depends upon the amount of information needed to understand the historical circumstances, and answer specific questions the pupil will ask of the evidence. At successive stages in a pupil's education from 8-18 the complexity of the contextual material builds up through the use of a range of secondary sources — textbooks, monographs, biographies and articles from history journals. As far as possible the framework should mirror the findings of academic historians in their work upon the topic concerned.

The second element in co-operative learning is the teacher's provision of a surrogate 'second record'. Historical thinking depends upon an adequate 'second record' to cope with the contextual framework and the evidence. Consequently the teacher's surrogate 'second record' provides clear guidelines along which the pupil can develop his understanding. Such guidelines involve a range of activities and questions which cover the spectrum of mental activity involved in the historian's work. Exercises fall into certain categories, which include:

1 Understanding the evidence: involving an explanation of contextual problems, e.g. historical references, names.
2 Questioning and assessment of the veracity and value of the source.
3 Handling the evidence to squeeze out the maximum understanding of the historical situation.
4 An understanding of the roles of the individuals and groups involved.
5 An understanding of the origins and possible development of the historical situation — so as to illustrate the historical concepts involved: cause, change, continuity and consequence.

The combination of a pattern of historical study, the ways in which written sources can be used at different levels as classroom resources, and the nature of co-operative learning means that pupils from 8-18 can engage meaningfully in the historical process. In certain areas by 18 they will be able to function as proto-historians.

(by Jon Nichol, from
Perspectives 4 — Developments in History Teaching)

Activity 6:
Resourcing history lessons

1 Obtain as wide a range as possible of resources used in your school to teach the youngest and the oldest age range, such as textbooks, archive units, pamphlets, slides, tapes and photographs. Then decide:
— which are primary and secondary sources for the study of history
— what steps has any historical evidence been through before it is used with children in the classroom

— what kind of knowledge is each resource being used for in the learning process: propositional (*know that*), procedural (*know how*), conceptual.

2 Use the observation schedule in Topic 12 to observe a history lesson or series of lessons for a first-year form being taught history for its first year. Then produce or suggest the resources you would use in the next lesson, and how you would go about making sure they were suited to the needs of the class.

Follow-up

1 Read the following, which deal with the questions of historical knowledge and historians and their evidence.

>Rogers, P.J., 1981, *The New History: theory into practice*, Historical Association, TH44. (An excellent analysis of the philosophical basis for teaching history, which is related to actual examples.)
>
>Palmer, M. and Batho, G.R., 1981, *The Source Method in History Teaching,* Historical Association, TH48. (A full explanation of both the theoretical and practical implications of teaching with resources.)
>
>Dickinson, A.K., Gard, A. and Lee, P.J., 1978, 'Evidence in history and the classroom' in Dickinson, A.K. and Lee, P.J. (eds), *History Teaching and Historical Understanding,* Heinemann. (A clear theoretical explanation of what is involved in the use of historical evidence in the classroom.)
>
>Pring, R., 1978, 'Philosophical Issues' in Lawton, D. et al. (eds), *Theory and Practice of Curriculum Studies,* Routledge & Kegan Paul. (A short account of the philosophical elements in educational knowledge.)

2 Begin to collect together a range of resources which might be useful in your history teaching.

**Topic 6
HISTORY OR
INTEGRATION?**

Children live in an integrated world. Subject boundaries are artificial, and merely reflect the archaic perpetuation of self-interested and self-indulgent academics in a university world divorced from the realities which face both staff and pupils in the real world of schools. Even if one accepts that the academic disciplines have a role to play, those at present taught in the humanities area are increasingly irrelevant. They have as much right to be in the curriculum as a course on medieval bee-keeping. History should be swept away and be replaced by a course built around the modern social sciences — sociology, anthropology and political studies.

Such are some of the arguments the integrationists advance. History teachers must be either capable of supporting their subject against such attacks, or if they are participating in an integrated course, put forward a positive role for their subject within the scheme proposed.

Integrated studies take a multitude of forms, and one problem of discussing integration is that there are so many different schemes available, and organising principles underlying them. It is first necessary to identify the subjects which are included in an integrated scheme — whether called humanities, social sciences, social or integrated studies. A common pattern is history and geography, but the integrationist net can encompass subjects as diverse as religious education, English, biology and chemistry.

If subjects are to be taught in an integrated way, a rationale must be produced to replace that which supports the teaching of the independent subjects. There are four nodal points upon which integrationists might base their schemes:

1 *Areas of knowledge* Education is concerned with developing within

each pupil eight complementary areas of knowledge. These eight areas are: the linguistic, the physical, the spiritual, the scientific, the mathematical, the social and political, the ethical, the aesthetic. Integrated studies should play a major role in developing the pupils' awareness in key areas such as the social and political, the ethical and the spiritual. The eight areas draw on all subjects.

2 *Teaching for skills* Education is concerned with developing a range of life skills which the pupil will need to cope with the modern world. The taxonomic approach (see Topic 3) clearly indicates the range and nature of the skills we need to foster. As the skills are common to all subjects, a curriculum scheme needs to be devised which draws upon the range of skills which the subjects can foster. A skills-based course provides a clear focus for the organisation of teaching, and is directly relevant to pupil needs.

3 *Teaching for concepts* All knowledge has a conceptual basis, and we should organise our teaching around these. Topic 4 outlines the kind of conceptual pattern which can successfully underlie an integrated studies course. A conceptual approach has the merit of being adaptable to the circumstances of each school, and provides a framework around which individual syllabi can be built.

4 *Integration and the curriculum* In terms of the school's overall pattern and social goals, integration is a sensible approach. A faculty system makes for more efficient management of the staff than through a plethora of single subjects. Teaching can be organised on a team or individual basis. If an individual teaches a form its whole programme of integrated studies (the common pattern), it means that the social interaction between teacher and pupils and between the pupils themselves is enhanced. The teacher's knowledge and understanding of the pupils must increase, and the pupils have the opportunity of learning in a much more flexible and varied manner than is possible under a traditional pattern of timetabling.

How can the history teacher cope with such an onslaught? History is a major resource area which can contribute to the integrated programme. Historical topics can be taught either separately, or as an element in supporting some area of knowledge, skill or skills or conceptual focus. The historian has a unique contribution to make in terms of the kinds of knowledge he or she can impart (see Topic 5), the relevance of the subject to the pupil's understanding (see Topic 2) and the range of skills which the historical process can foster (see Topics 3 and 4). The sociologist's claim to be the standard bearer of enlightenment and truth is not proven, and Derek Heater has some thought-provoking ideas:

There are subjects that have clearly defined structures — the subjects, indeed, whose very *raison d'être* is the formulation of general laws. And here, surely, lies a vitally important distinction between history and the social sciences. The fact that sociology and its neighbouring disciplines are pretenders to the title of 'science' places them in the category of structured subjects analysable into basic concepts, which in turn may be built into a Brunerian spiral. History, on the other hand, is primarily concerned with the uniqueness of events (*pace* Arnold Toynbee) rather than recurring patterns. To those who would argue that they have, in fact, discovered historical concepts I would answer that these concepts are either social science concepts (e.g. class, leadership) or that they are non-transferable descriptions (e.g. the Reformation) which, however useful they may be as 'containers' of certain historical information, are unique to the historical situation under review and therefore irrelevant to the task of constructing a spiral syllabus.

The denial to history of discrete constituent concepts is by no means intended as a denial of its value as a subject for study. On the contrary, I would wish to argue that history is *more* than a subject (in the usual, timetable meaning of this term and in the sense that economics, for example, is a subject); and furthermore that a clearer understanding of what is probably the most natural relationship between this broadly conceived history and the social science subjects would lead easily to a coherent curriculum in this sphere. My argument is as follows. History should be perceived not merely as a subject, but rather as a mode of thought: all subjects can be studied historically. Nevertheless, history has traditionally been used particularly as a means of social and political education, with consequent emphasis on the social and political aspects of history; the histories of science and art, for example, have rarely featured in any important way in syllabuses. If the argument has been sound up to this point, the conclusion that one must draw is surely that history should be taught in such a way that it is used as a vehicle for the basic social science concepts. The social sciences, in other words, will be used as ways of articulating the historical mode of thought.

(from Heater, D., 1970, 'History and the Social Sciences' in Ballard, M. (ed.), *New Movements in the Study and Teaching of History*, Temple Smith.)

Activity 7: Integrating history

1 If your school has an integrated studies course, obtain the rationale which the department will have produced when framing it and which they give new members of the humanities team. Under the four headings: areas of knowledge, teaching for skills, teaching for concepts, integration and the curriculum, make out a list of the ways in which your integrated scheme matches the ideas presented at the beginning of this Topic.

2 Analyse a week's teaching of a humanities form in the first year the scheme is taught in your, or a neighbouring, school, to see how the principles underlying integration appear to be carried out *in practice*.

Follow-up

1 Draw up your own scheme for teaching integrated studies/humanities in your school, with sample material for teaching a week's lessons in the course. To help you with your outline, consult the following:

Warwick, D. (ed.), 1973, *Integrated Studies in the Secondary school*, Hodder and Stoughton. (An excellent analysis of the range of integrated studies found in schools, plus case studies.)

Lawton, D. and Dufour, B., 1973, *The New Social Studies*, Heinemann. (A masterly survey of the whole field.)

Blyth, A. et al., 1976, *Place, Time and Society 8-13: Curriculum planning in history, geography and social sciences*, Collins, ESL.

**Topic 7
THINKING IN HISTORY**

Your history teaching should be based upon one axiom: all children can *think*. Recent research suggests that given the right materials and teaching environment pupils of all ages can think in a variety of ways, and can function at a relatively sophisticated conceptual level. History teachers no longer believe the findings of the 1960s and 70s that children's historical thinking lagged severely behind their thinking in other subjects, and that it was fruitless to engage upon any serious historical study before the age of 16.

In developing their thinking children need to use a range of resources carefully prepared for their use, and to be given tasks appropriate to their abilities. The material below, from the introduction to a text book for twelve and thirteen-year-olds, is typical. The exercise is only concerned with encouraging the pupils to think about immediately observable features of the picture. It does not deal with topics such as the nature and provenance of the source, the relationship of the picture to the rest of the tapestry, the purpose for which the tapestry was woven and what other things the picture can tell us about the Norman age. The author's aim was simply to stimulate interest and thinking about a topic of which the pupils have some knowledge.

INTRODUCTION

THE NORMANS provides an outline course on the Norman age, and its impact on Britain and Europe. Pages 2-31 examine the main themes: how the Normans conquered Britain; settled in parts of Europe; went on crusades, and ruled their lands.

Pages 32-64 examine different aspects of Norman life and society, and allow a deeper study of subjects introduced in the first half of the book.

Throughout THE NORMANS emphasis is laid upon the handling of historical EVIDENCE. Each subject encourages the pupil to think actively about the clues the past has left behind, and on the basis of the evidence to work out his own ideas about the Normans.

The book is carefully arranged for class, group or individual work. Each subject is self-contained, and provides material for topic work. The questions are roughly graded for difficulty, and give scope for pupils who work at different speeds. They are carefully designed to encourage pupils to think about, and so build up their own picture of, the past.

"Here Harold the King was killed."

History is made up from EVIDENCE from the past – a debate between sources. Look at one such historical CLUE, **A,** about how Harold, King of England, died at the Battle of Hastings in 1066. Most historians believe that Harold was killed by an arrow through his eye. How do you think Harold was killed? Look carefully at **A,** and think about **a, b** and **c**.

a Is Harold supposed to be the man below the word HAROLD? Or, is he the man falling to the ground below the words WAS KILLED?

b A is from the Bayeux Tapestry. The tapestry is the *only* clue from the Norman age that an arrow may have hit Harold in the eye.

c Historians think that needlewomen wove the tapestry about twenty years after the Battle of Hastings, probably in Britain.

Now how do you think Harold was killed?

Before reading pages 2-3, write down what you know about the Normans.

(from Jon Nichol, 1980, *The Normans*, Basil Blackwell.)

**Activity 8:
Thinking in history**

The nature and sophistication of pupils' thinking vary greatly. One approach is to look at pupils' work in relation to various cognitive levels.

1   By yourself, in pairs or as members of a group, answer the question: How do you think Harold was killed? Then analyse your answers according to the following criteria:

Levels of historical thinking

- A   Conclusion linked to *one* piece of given evidence. E.g., An arrow hit Harold in the eye.
- B   Conclusion linked to *two* pieces of given evidence. E.g., Harold could be the man with the arrow in his eye or the one being cut down by the man on horseback.
- C   Conclusion linked to *three* pieces of given evidence.
- D   Conclusion(s) linked to *external general knowledge.* E.g., The picture shows a battle.
- E   Conclusion(s) linked to *external general historical knowledge* plus D. E.g., The picture shows knights in chain mail, using battleaxes, broadswords, etc.
- F   Conclusion(s) linked to *sophisticated historical knowledge.* E.g., The picture shows the Battle of Hastings. King Harold has just marched from the Battle of Stamford Bridge with his housecarls, and is facing the invading force of Duke William of Normandy, made up from . . .
- G   Conclusion(s) linked to *sophisticated historical knowledge* and *questioning of the evidence.* E.g., The picture is taken from the Bayeux tapestry. Its accuracy is open to doubt as it was woven twenty years later on the orders of Odo of Bayeux etc. The picture shows a typical Saxon fighting formation, with the shield wall encircling the position. The figure in the wall with an arrow in the eye is likely to be a housecarl, while the central knight being struck down is more likely to be Harold . . .
- H   Conclusion(s) linked to *detailed knowledge of sources.* The Bayeux tapestry seems to have been based upon William of Poitiers' account of the battle, although William does not mention the way in which Harold died.

Follow-up

Much of the work into the ways in which children's historical thinking and understanding develops relate to the findings of Jean Piaget. In the 1960s and 1970s Piaget's findings were used to analyse children's historical thinking – see Hallam, R.N. (1970). Subsequently Hallam's views have been widely discounted – see Booth, M., in *Teaching History*, No 21, June 1978, and Dickinson, A.K. and Lee, P.J. (eds) (1978).

Look at the following. As you read each, think of what it suggests about: how children think in history, how the lessons of the research should be applied to our history lessons and what is wrong with the findings – i.e. do you think the conclusions are sound, do the tests seem sensible?

Steele, I., 1976, *Developments in History Teaching.* (A very clear introduction.)

R.N. Hallam, 'Piaget and Thinking in History' in Ballard, M. (ed.), 1970.

M. Booth, 'Children's Inductive Historical Thought', *Teaching History*, No 21, June 1978.

A.K. Dickinson and P.J. Lee, 1978, 'Explanation and Understanding in History' and 'Understanding and Research' in Dickinson, A.K. and Lee, P.J., (eds).

**Topic 8
NEW IDEAS IN HISTORY**

Recent changes in history teaching are loosely known as 'The New History'. What does it involve? The *Schools Council Project History 13-16* (see Denis Shemilt's article below) has been seminal. The introductions to two new series of textbooks for pupils in the 9-14 and 11-16 age range respectively suggest how the New History has been translated into classroom practice.

**Activity 9:
Innovating in history teaching**

1   Discuss the ways in which you were taught history at school; what were the distinguishing features?

2   How different was the way in which you were taught from the approach outlined in:
— The Schools Council Project 'History 13-16'
— Macmillan's *History in the Making* series
— Blackwell's *Evidence* series

3   Use the information in the Shemilt article, and your reading from Topic 1, to draw up a list of the features you think the New History teaching contains.

Changes in the teaching of history over the last decade have raised many problems, to which there are no easy solutions. The classification of objectives, the presentation of material in varied and appropriate language, the use and abuse of evidence and the reconsideration of assessment techniques are four of the more important. Many teachers are now encouraging their pupils individually or in groups to participate in the processes and skills of the professional historian. Moreover such developments are being discussed increasingly in the context of mixed ability classes and the need to provide suitable teaching approaches for them.

History in the Making is a new course for secondary schools intended for pupils of average ability. It is a contribution to the current debate, and provides one possible way forward. It accepts many of the proven virtues of traditional courses: the fascination of the good tale, the drama of human life, individual and collective, the need to provide a visual stimulus to support the written word.

But it has built on to these some of the key features of the 'new history' so that teachers can explore, within the framework of a text book, many of the 'new' approaches and techniques.

To this end each chapter in this volume has four major components.

1   *The text*   This provides the basic framework of the chapters, and although the approach is essentially factual, it is intended to arouse and sustain the interest of the reader of average ability.

2   *The illustrations*   These have been carefully selected to stand beside the written pieces of evidence in the chapter, and to provide (so far as is possible) an authentic visual image of the period/topic. Photographs, artwork and maps are all used to clarify and support the text, and to develop the pupil's powers of observation.

3   *Using the evidence*   This is a detailed study of the evidence on one particular aspect of the chapter. Did the Walls of Jericho really come tumbling down? Was the death of William Rufus in the New Forest really an accident? What was the background to the torpedoing of the *Lusitania*? These are the sort of questions which are asked, to give the pupil the opportunity to consider not only the problems facing the historian, but also those facing the characters of history. Different forms of documentary evidence are considered, as well as archaeological, architectural, statistical, and other kinds of source material; the intention is to give the pupil a genuine, if modest, insight into the making of history.

4   *Questions and further work*   These are intended to test and develop the pupil's reading of the chapter, in particular the *Using the Evidence* section. Particular attention is paid to the development of historical skills, through the examination and interpretation of evidence. The differences between primary and secondary sources, for example, are explored, and concepts such as bias in evidence introduced through specific examples. Some comprehension questions are included, but the emphasis is very much on involving

pupils with the materials, and helping them to develop a critical awareness of different kinds of evidence and its limitations. By applying the skills which they have developed, pupils may then be able to formulate at a suitable level and in appropriate language, ideas and hypotheses of their own.

History in the Making is a complete course in five volumes, to meet the needs of pupils between the ages of 11 and 16 (in other words up to and including the first public examination). However each volume stands by itself and may be used independently of the others; given the variety of syllabuses in use in schools today this flexibility is likely to be welcomed by many teachers. *The Ancient World* and *The Medieval World* are intended primarily for 11-13-year-old pupils, *The Early Modern World, 1450-1700* for 12-14-year-old pupils, *Britain, Europe and Beyond, 1700-1900* for pre-CSE pupils and *The Twentieth Century* for CSE examination candidates.

It is our hope that pupils will be encouraged, within the main topics and themes of British, European and World History, to experience for themselves the stimulus and challenge, the pleasure and frustration, the vitality and humanity that are an essential part of History in the Making.

(from J.A.P. Jones, 1979, *History in the Making*, Macmillan)

SCHOOLS COUNCIL PROJECT 'HISTORY 13-16': PAST, PRESENT AND FUTURE

'I cannot give the reasons,
I only sing the tunes'.
      (Mervyn Peake)

In 1972 the Schools Council founded the 'History 13-16' Project in response to the manifest opportunities offered by the New History movement and the challenges perceived in the waxing influence of integrated and social science subjects on the secondary school curriculum. The Project's shape and nature were largely dictated by the remit laid down by the History Subject Committee of Schools Council. The three most critical elements in this remit were the injunctions:

(i)   to base the Project around public examinations at 16+;
(ii)   to consider the position of History within 'the whole curriculum';
(iii) to ground innovation in the most radical and workable practice current in schools.

The sum of these requirements specified a journeyman project composed from existing realities and aspirations, and more closely geared to current classroom options and constraints than to educational theories and ideals. It had to be sufficiently novel and radical to offer teachers the opportunity for genuine innovation, without being so bizarre and alien as to constitute a high risk with all-important examination classes.

A survey of existing classroom practice conducted 1972-73 persuaded the Project team that the overriding priority was to provide an alternative rationale for upper secondary history, not with a view to supplanting the traditional model, but solely to afford teachers a genuine choice as to the sort of History that they wished to pursue. As far as methods were concerned, it seemed necessary to start with whatever aspects of conventional classroom practice seemed best suited to the new rationale and to then encourage the emergence of more radical and Project-specific techniques if experience proved this necessary. The Project syllabus, materials and examinations, were thus seen as a framework within which curriculum innovation and experiment could proceed. They were not seen as a blueprint for success, a recipe for good practice.

Project Rationale

The rationale of 'History 13-16' has two planks: first, History must meet adolescent needs if it is to warrant inclusion in the secondary curriculum; and second, the subject should be taught as an 'approach to knowledge' rather than as a 'body of knowledge'.

The project team isolated five adolescent needs potentially answerable by a study of History:

'1. The need to understand the world in which they live.
2. The need to find their personal identity by widening their experience through the study of people of a different time and place.
3. The need to understand the process of change and continuity in human affairs.
4. The need to begin to acquire leisure interests.
5. The need to develop the ability to think critically, and to make judgements about human situations'.

(*A New Look at History*, p. 12)

The second strand in Project philosophy, the emphasis upon the subject as an 'approach to knowledge' rather than a 'body of content' derived first and foremost from the need to justify History as a worthwhile pursuit for the majority of adolescents whose acquaintance with the subject would terminate at the age 14 or 16 years. 'If one of the functions of schools is to show the next generation what pursuits adults have found valuable and worthwhile, then it is important to make a conscious attempt to show pupils what history is. Similarly it is the job of the teacher to introduce pupils to the language and meanings which have been developed over the years and which historians share and use. This is obviously true for pupils who will go on to study more history, but it is also particularly important for pupils who will not. If they leave school without any understanding of what history is, it is unlikely that they will either find their own interests in the historical field or have much sympathy or tolerance for those who do'. (*A New Look at History*, p. 22.)

Secondary History, it was argued, should be 'progressive' in that it makes equal sense to terminate or continue study at or beyond the traditional break-points of fourteen and sixteen years. This claim is difficult to make for traditional content-based History. How do you justify an 'outline' that stops at the Tudors? And is there not something odd about an outline overview founded upon an eleven-year-old's memories of Norman Britain and capped with a sixteen-year-old's conceptions of Adolf Hitler? These questions and others persuaded the Project team that while historical content would remain the indispensable substance of any course, it could not, of itself, supply the raison d'être for the subject's retention in the secondary curriculum.

Syllabus, Materials and Assessment

The course is in two parts: an examination course to 'O' Level and CSE, and an introductory course for thirteen-year-old pupils. The latter, entitled 'What Is History?' consists of five units of materials focused upon the subject matter of history (people in the past), the historian's claim to know (clues, types of evidence, problems with evidence), and the historian's concern to question and explain (motivation and causation).

The examination course has four discrete segments, each of which is supported by a variety of pupil and teacher materials.

Mode 1 'O' Level and CSE examinations are offered nationally by the SUIB and SREB. A single syllabus and assessment pattern are common to these examinations, thus allowing CSE and GCE candidates to be taught in mixed groups. Commonality apart, the most radical feature of the assessment is a 90-minute-long methods paper using unseen source materials relating to a topic or topics not previously studied. This carries 30 per cent of the total mark allocation. A second paper, of two hours duration, is based upon the taught syllabus. This too carries 30 per cent of the total assessment. The remaining 40 per cent of marks is devoted to course-work.

Alarums and Excursions

The unseen methods paper and the discontinuous syllabus have been viewed as more radical developments than the 'approach to knowledge' rationale and attempt to answer adolescent needs. Such opposition and scepticism as the Project attracts usually centres upon one or both of these features.

Project teachers have found the segmented syllabus useful in motivating pupils, and no serious problems have been reported. But the discontinuous pill has proved too bitter for some to swallow, and fears have been expressed that a 'bits-and-pieces' course will result in pupils failing to grasp the idea of 'continuity' essential to any understanding of historical narrative. There is no evidence that these fears are well founded. On the contrary, the Project evaluation suggests that Project pupils develop a more sophisticated grasp of 'change' and 'continuity' than do pupils following traditional courses. (This finding is not as surprising as may first appear: traditional continuous syllabuses are usually taught as a series of discrete topics, especially when teachers question spot, and one segment of the Project course, the Study in Development, is explicitly concerned with questions of change and continuity in history.)

The unseen methods paper, it has been objected, is 'artificial' and 'unhistorical'. Historians, the argument runs, would never use sources out of context. This is perfectly true but misses the point. Implicit in this line of argument is the suggestion that we can only assess mastery and understanding of historical method by 'non-artificial' means, by having pupils 'do what historians do'. This is disingenuous in the extreme. The research thesis has its place, but not in the secondary school. An assessment technique should be judged on whether or not it allows judgements to be made about what pupils understand and do not understand, can and cannot do. It should not be judged by the degree to which it mirrors, or seems to mirror, the activities of professional historians. Ironically in view of the criticism received from some quarters, the unseen methods paper has proved to be the most demonstrably valid of the three assessment modes employed.

Present Status of 'History 13-16'

Take-up apart, Project impact is difficult to quantify, and even with take-up it is necessary to distinguish the use of Project materials as general resources from full-scale implementation of the course. National sales figures and the occasional l.e.a. census suggest the third-year course to have been purchased in quantity by between 40 per cent and 50 per cent of English secondary schools, and examination course materials to be widely used in 30 per cent of schools. Statistics for operations of the entire three-year package are far more modest. In September 1979, the Project constituency was certainly in excess of 11 per cent and almost certainly below 15 per cent of English secondary schools. Take-up in Northern Ireland is more modest, but highly respectable. Penetration of Welsh and Scottish schools is virtually non-existent.

Wider impact is difficult to demonstrate insofar as developments consistent with Project philosophy cannot necessarily be attributed to the Project's example. Nonetheless, three publishing houses have explicitly indicated a desire to incorporate the lessons of 'History 13-16' into new series planned for the 11-14 age group, and two other publishers have produced materials remarkably convergent with Project philosophy and practice. Impact upon publishing aimed at the 14-16 age group has been minimal. One publisher has successfully competed with the Project's own MWS materials, but this is an attempt to break into the 'History 13-16' market rather than to infiltrate its ideals and methods into traditional courses. Until examination boards radically change the syllabuses on offer, publishing for the 14-16 age group is likely to remain fairly conservative.

Although no boards have explicitly acknowledged debts to Project philosophy and assessment experience, a number of 'O'Level and CSE boards are currently experimenting with unseen methods papers. Even if patrilineal descent cannot be proved, the Project's role in resolving several technical problems and winning a measure of public acceptance for methods papers is unlikely to have gone unnoticed by board panels and research departments.

More significant, if less tangible, is the Project's role in the recent reassessment of what children are capable of achieving in History.

(by D.J. Shemilt from *History Teaching Review*, April 1980, Vol. 12. 1.)

Follow-up

1 Your school will have been sent a range of educational publishers' catalogues. Ask the head of the history department, or the humanities head, for up-to-date copies and send off for inspection copies of the most interesting titles that are not already in the school.

When the books arrive, make out a table putting them into the order in which you would like to use them for the appropriate age ranges, with your reasons.

2 Read through back numbers of *Teaching History*, and discuss any interesting ideas and suggestions the articles might contain. In particular read:

Barker, B., 'History Situations', 1977, *Teaching History*, no. 17. This article has had a profound impact on the way in which many teachers view their history teaching.

**Topic 9
SCHOOL ORGANISATION**

It is important to find out how your new, or current, school is organised and run, as this will have a big influence upon your teaching. In particular, think about the kind of knowledge which the school is trying to impart. Look closely for the hidden curriculum — the range of ideas, attitudes and opinions which the school conveys to the pupil, but which are not part of the formal curriculum. In curriculum terms it is vital to place your history teaching against a wider context of learning in the humanities, the school's language policy and the general patterns of learning experienced in other areas and faculties.

**Activity 10:
Looking at school organisation**

Carry out a survey of the school to which you are attached, using the following headings:

1 *Composition* — size (number of pupils), sex ratio, age range, ability range, social background, geographical background (size of catchment area).

2 *Organisation of staff* — head, deputy heads and functions, heads of year/ house-heads (pastoral), heads of faculty, heads of departments, size of departments.

3 *Organisation of pupils* — houses, mini-houses, forms.

4 *The timetable* — how is the teaching day organised? What form does the options scheme take at the end of year three?

5 *The curriculum* — what is the curriculum at different levels in the school? You may find there is a major division between the lower school (up to the age of 14), the 14-16 age range and the 16-19 students. Are there any clear curriculum aims for the whole school?

6 *Teaching patterns* — how does the school organise its teaching — is it mixed ability, banded, streamed? Does this change from year to year, and does it vary from subject to subject? Is it different *in practice* from what it claims to be? For example, through the options system at 14+ is there 'de facto' banding and streaming?

7 *The headteacher's role* — examine the way in which the headteacher runs the school, and the attitude and feelings towards him or her.

8 *Ethos* — what is the general 'feel' of the school? How successfully does the ethos reflect the school's general and specific goals?

9   Does the school have a language policy? If so, what?

10   How well do you think you fit into the school? After carrying out your survey, what changes in attitude and behaviour might you make?

Follow-up

It is vital to try to find out what makes a successful school. Read the following, and then say how the reading has changed your perception of the school you surveyed in this Activity.

Rutter, M. et al., 1979, *Fifteen Thousand Hours*, Open Books.

Dancy, J. (ed.), 1980, *Perspectives 1 – The Rutter Research*, School of Education, University of Exeter. (*Perspectives* 1 is obtainable from: The Curriculum and Resources Centre, University of Exeter School of Education, St. Luke's, Exeter, EX1 2LU.)

Topic 10
THE HISTORY DEPARTMENT

Activity 11:
Examining the history department

Your teaching will largely depend upon how the history department is run. An examination of your department will often reveal a range of resources and materials of which you were unaware.

Use the following points to sort out the organisation of the history department.

What is the history department?

1   How many people are there in the department (names, ages, interests, etc.)?

2   What are their functions – i.e. what jobs do they do within the department? Note the relationship between their history teaching role and their other functions, such as work within other disciplines and in the humanities area in general, or their more general school role as heads of year, etc.

3   What is the structure of history teaching within the school – i.e. number of lessons per week for each group, nature of the teaching groups, examination demands?

4   What is the history curriculum, and how does this relate to the school curriculum (see Topic 9)? Lower School, 11-14, CSE/'O' level, non-examination, upper school/'A' level/general studies?

5   The state of the history rooms, and equipment. Make an inventory of what is available for: video; slides/filmstrips; tapes/cassettes; archive units and resource kits; textbooks; books, pamphlets, etc; home produced resources.

6   How are the department's resources organised?

Follow-up

Use your analysis of 'What is the history department?' as a basis for building up your own resources and teaching aids and materials. If you feel there are major shortages, bring these to the notice of the departmental head, and suggest at a departmental meeting that purchases might be made in these areas.

At the end of your study period carry out Activity 18, which allows for a much more thorough survey of the history department.

**Topic 11
PROBLEMS OF CLASS MANAGEMENT**

Managing a class is rather like driving a car. Riding with an experienced driver makes it seem easy and simple – until you try for yourself for the first time. The transport of delight turns into a vehicle of nightmares, with the grinding of machinery and an erratic and often near-fatal course. Learning to drive needs expert tuition, and so does class management. Below is a list of advice given by experienced teachers to help students. In a Teacher Education Project study (Wragg, 1981) the students said they found the advice most useful in helping them to manage their classes.

TIPS GIVEN TO STUDENTS

Students were asked which of the general teaching tips they had been given had proved to be most helpful. They had received these from tutors, teachers, friends, books, even pupils. The most common 25 tips are given below.

1. start by being firm with pupils: you can relax later
2. get silence before you start speaking to the class
3. control the pupils' entry to the classroom
4. know and use the pupils' names
5. prepare lessons thoroughly and structure them firmly
6. arrive at the classroom before the pupils
7. prepare furniture and apparatus before the pupils arrive
8. know how to use apparatus and be familiar with experiments before you use them in class
9. be mobile and walk around the class
10. start the lesson with a 'bang' and sustain interest and curiosity
11. give clear instructions
12. learn voice control
13. have additional material prepared to cope, e.g. with bright and slow pupils' needs
14. look at the class when speaking, and learn to scan
15. make written work appropriate (e.g. to the age, ability, cultural background of pupils)
16. develop an effective questioning technique
17. develop the art of timing to fit the available period
18. vary your teaching technique
19. anticipate discipline problems and act quickly
20. be firm and consistent in giving punishments
21. avoid confrontations
22. clarify and insist on your standards
23. don't patronise pupils; treat them as responsible beings
24. show yourself as a helper or facilitator to the pupils
25. use humour constructively.

Tips are useful, but when you are managing a class you often have to deal with serious problems. Below are some of the things which have happened to me in my teaching career.

(a) You are teaching a second-year remedial group. There has been a staff meeting at break. You arrive twenty minutes late for the lesson. Two boys are fighting, a boy and girl are crawling around under the desks, and two boys are reading a pornographic magazine.

(b) You have been teaching a CSE/'O' level group World History. A group of pupils come to you and say they are bored to death and feel that you are wasting their time.

(c) You have a lively and interesting CSE/'O' level group, with the exception of one boy. He refuses to co-operate, makes rude noises, interrupts and generally poisons the classroom atmosphere. This pupil disrupts all the lessons he is in, and has driven the French teacher to the brink of a nervous breakdown.

(d) You are giving a lesson which depends on the use of slides. The lesson starts, and the projector bulb blows. There is no spare.

(e) The department has run out of stationery, and it is halfway through the summer term. Two pupils ask you for new exercise books.

Activity 12:
Managing the history lesson

1   Put the 25 'tips' outlined in the box into what you consider the order of importance for successful classroom management. Make notes to explain the reasons behind your order.

2   Discuss each of the incidents (a)-(e). How would you have coped with the situations described?

Follow-up

1   Observe the teaching of a *successful* history teacher, and note each time he or she uses one of the techniques listed. Then analyse the lesson as a whole and think why his or her management was successful.

2   Ask an experienced teacher to put the list into his or her own order of importance. Then consider why this order differs from yours.

3   Give the list to a form to put into what it considers the order of importance. Then think about the differences between their order and yours.

Topic 12
LESSON OBSERVATION

Lesson observation is a tremendous help in getting you to improve your own teaching. I first realised the glaring inadequacies of my own teaching when I observed the classroom performances of others — both good and bad lessons. The danger of observation is to do it in a passive, non-analytical manner. Admiring the view or anything else that takes your fancy might be fun, but it doesn't help your teaching. You need to be positive, and apply the lessons you learn to your own teaching.

Activity 13:
Observing history teaching

Obtain permission to observe an experienced teacher taking a class for a series of lessons. In the lessons observed make rough notes about some of the important activities and skills outlined below. For each lesson make out a separate table:

class: ability level:
topic:
resources (books, etc.):

1   Lesson beginning

2   Transitions from one activity to another

3   Lesson ending

4   Explanations and instructions

5   Questioning

6   Pitch and pace of teacher talk

7   Whole class teaching (duration, nature)

8   Group work

9   Individual work

The key element in teaching is how the teacher relates to the pupils and communicates to the class on either a class, group or individual level. Throughout the lesson pay particular attention to pupil-teacher interaction, and how the teacher communicates. Use the following headings to make notes, which you can write up later:

1   Language level of the teacher (is it appropriate to the classroom situation?)
2   Non-verbal interactions
3   Variety of approach
4   Planning of teacher's time (time spent on different activities)
5   Appropriateness of content and materials

Follow-up

1   If possible, discuss the lesson with the teacher, in particular to see whether he or she felt he/she had achieved his/her aims and objectives.

2   Compare and discuss your notes with those of colleagues who sat in on other lessons.

3   Compare the periods on which you have made notes. What lessons have you learned for application to your own teaching?

**Topic 13
READY, STEADY, GO —
QUIZ TIME!**

Have you done the following, or mastered the skills indicated? If so, you will be fully prepared to teach history.

	YES	NO

1 Use of items of equipment.
   Can you use with confidence a
   ... slide projector
   ... overhead projector
   ... banda machine
   ... cassette tape recorder
   ... reel-to-reel tape recorder
   ... radio set for using with schools broadcasts
   ... television set — the school model
   ... videotape recorder
   ... Apple/BBC 2/Sinclair Spectrum/Commodore Pet or Research Machine 380Z computer?

2 Have you a clear strategy for teaching mixed or wide range ability classes?

3 Do you have a full knowledge of the resources available for history teaching in the school?

4 Are you clear about where you can get the resources you will need to teach in the way you think appropriate?

5 For your exam forms, have you got:
   ... a breakdown of topics to teach
   ... time allowed for each topic
   ... a selection of back papers
   ... full knowledge of the syllabus?

6 Have you a stock cupboard key? (vital!)

7 Have you a *teacher survival kit* containing the following:
   ... chalks, white, coloured
   ... blackboard cleaner or duster
   ... bottle of blackboard cleaning fluid
   ... bottle of water for cleaning *white* boards which use felt pens
   ... felt pens for use with *white* board
   ... felt pens for use with o.h.p.
   ... 6 pencils to lend pupils
   ... 6 rubbers to lend pupils
   ... 6 ball-point pens to lend pupils
   ... penknife or pencil sharpener
   ... wristwatch or stopwatch?

8 Do you know how or when you can get stationery you may need, e.g. tracing paper, graph paper, exercise books, plain paper, etc.?

9 Have you a clear idea about record keeping in history?

Part 2   TEACHING HISTORY

In this part of the workbook you are invited to scrutinise your own teaching through a series of eleven structured exercises. You should also ask a colleague to help you, where appropriate, by observing your teaching. For students, the presence of an observer is a normal occurrence and you may use either a tutor or another student to help you. Experienced teachers get out of the habit of being observed in the classroom. But it is useful to undertake this kind of 'observational pairing' either with another member of an in-service course or with a member of your own, or even another, department. Tackle the eleven exercises in order if you can. If not, then make a selection about the sequence and priorities you wish to adopt in the light of your own needs and circumstances. Attention is focused in this section on:

... the daily life of the history teacher
... lesson planning
... managing skill
... discussion leadership
... teacher-pupil interactions
... handling concepts
... questioning
... individual pupils
... slow learners
... handling classroom groups

Focus 1
A DAY IN THE LIFE OF A HISTORY TEACHER

What to do: If you are a student, arrange to spend the whole of *one* day with a history teacher. If you are teaching, keep a log of how you spend your time. During the day concentrate on the range of tasks he or she has to carry out. This Focus contains two elements, a diary of the day and a log for analysis of the use of resources.

Section A   The Diary

Make out a diary with full details of *everything* (within reason) that the teacher does in the school during the teaching day. It might begin:

8.50   Arrives at staffroom, reads mail and notes, discusses problems of a deviant member of the class with the tutor responsible for pastoral care.

8.55   Goes to form room. Takes register. Collects bus money for the history trip. Forwards letter concerning child's absence to pastoral tutor.

9.00   Collects exercise books from stock room. Form goes to assembly. Accompanies them.

9.10   Lesson one — first-year mixed ability on Caesar's invasion of Britain.

9.12   Arrival of the tutor to discuss problems of one of the pupils.

9.15   Recommences teaching.

9.20   Pupil from another class asks for keys to stock cupboard ...

And so on, until the end of the school day. You could ask whether the teacher will be doing any reading/preparation/marking in the evening.

Section B The Use of Resources

During the day the teacher will employ a range of resources. Find out and note down the following information about the teacher's work.

(a) *Textbooks* Which textbooks are used? For each, note how it is used; how suitable you think both the teacher and pupils found it.

(b) *Worksheets and workcards* How often were these used? (Was the day 'death by a thousand workcards' for the pupils?)
What kinds of worksheets/cards are used — are they produced commercially, or in the school?
Are they individual (teacher) material, or part of the departmental stock?
How are they designed? Are they legible? Do they efficiently do the job for which they were intended?
Carry out a readability test on two sample cards or sheets. Use the procedure outlined below.

(c) *Blackboard technique* How and when does the teacher use the blackboard? How effective as a technique is it?

(d) *Audio-visual* Describe what visual aids were used in the course of the day, and their effectiveness.

(e) *Teacher talk* Try to assess the relative use of this technique as a method of imparting information.

Readability Test — or lost in the smog . . .

Select three written passages. Each passage should contain *ten* sentences. For the set of thirty sentences find 'p', the number of words with *three* or more syllables. Make sure you know what a syllable is!

The SMOG formula is:

reading age = $N + 8$
To find N, follow this procedure:

$$N = \sqrt{p}$$
$$p = \underline{} + \underline{} + \underline{}$$

For example, if in the three passages, omitting titles and quotations, there are 18, 30 and 21 three-syllable words, respectively,

$p = 18 + 30 + 21$ (total = 69)
$N = \sqrt{69}$ (8 is nearest square root)
∴ reading age = $8 + 8$
  = 16

Follow-up

1 At the end of the day consider what you think are the main features of the *teacher's style*, and how he or she has adapted his/her techniques to the range of demands made upon him/her. Also, analyse the teacher's functions into teaching and non-teaching demands.

2 For more detailed information on analysing the teacher's day, consult:

Hilsum, S. and Strong, C., 1978, *The Secondary Teacher's Day*, National Foundation for Educational Research.
Hilsum, S. and Crane, B.S., 1973, *The Teacher's Day*, NFER (for the primary and junior teacher's day).

Focus 2
LESSON PLANNING

What to do: Teaching is a science, and the lessons are experiments. Good teaching depends upon careful thought and the development of a wide range of skills. Systematic long- and short-term planning of lessons plays a major part in this.

1 Plan out your term's teaching for a particular class along the lines suggested below.
2 Make sure that you have planned in *detail* your lessons for the next week.

Lesson Planning Each lesson should be planned to allow for the maximum amount of effective learning. Too rigid or too slack a framework can be either restrictive or counter-productive, and the art of lesson planning is to strike a balance. Each individual lesson plan should relate to:

(a) The overall aims and objectives of the course
(b) The teaching timetable you have either laid down or are required to follow
(c) The pattern of teaching you have developed in your work with the class
(d) Your immediate experience of the class.

Inside the lesson you should think about maintaining as high a level of pupil involvement and activity as possible. Lessons break down into separate sections. Inside the overall pattern of introduction, body of lesson, and conclusion/finishing, you will embark upon a range of activities. Think carefully of the teaching relationship and pattern you expect from *each* such activity, and plan each around the pattern of transition — introduction — activity — resolution — introduction etc.

The following flow chart shows what is involved, and should be an aid to your planning.

Follow the arrows and cross your fingers. Yes – I know the answer, No – I don't know the answer, or am not sure, or cannot.

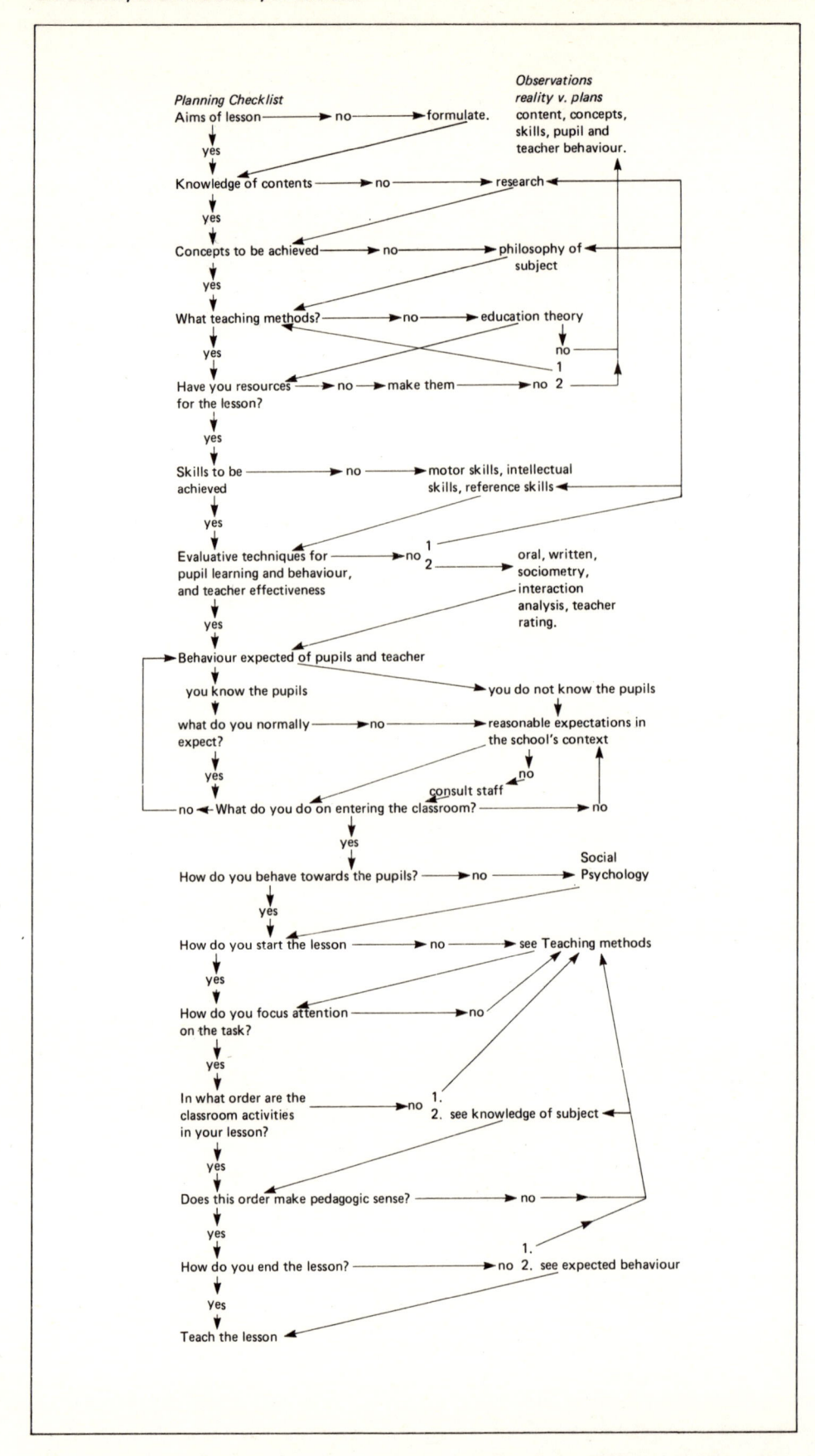

Planning Checklist

Aims of lesson ⟶ no ⟶ formulate.
↓ yes

Knowledge of contents ⟶ no ⟶ research
↓ yes

Concepts to be achieved ⟶ no ⟶ philosophy of subject
↓ yes

What teaching methods? ⟶ no ⟶ education theory
↓ yes

Have you resources ⟶ no ⟶ make them ⟶ no
for the lesson?
↓ yes

Skills to be achieved ⟶ no ⟶ motor skills, intellectual skills, reference skills
↓ yes

Evaluative techniques for pupil learning and behaviour, and teacher effectiveness ⟶ no 1, 2 ⟶ oral, written, sociometry, interaction analysis, teacher rating.
↓ yes

Observations
reality v. plans content, concepts, skills, pupil and teacher behaviour.

Behaviour expected of pupils and teacher
  you know the pupils   you do not know the pupils
         ↓   ↓
what do you normally ⟶ no ⟶ reasonable expectations in
expect?   the school's context
         ↓ yes   ↓ no
                              consult staff
no ⟵ What do you do on entering the classroom? ⟶ no
         ↓ yes

How do you behave towards the pupils? ⟶ no ⟶ Social Psychology
↓ yes

How do you start the lesson ⟶ no ⟶ see Teaching methods
↓ yes

How do you focus attention on the task? ⟶ no
↓ yes

In what order are the classroom activities in your lesson? ⟶ no 1. 2. see knowledge of subject
↓ yes

Does this order make pedagogic sense? ⟶ no
↓ yes

How do you end the lesson? ⟶ no 1. 2. see expected behaviour
↓ Yes

Teach the lesson

(This lesson planning chart is reproduced from H. Busher, 1980, 'The development of the lesson planning chart', *Teaching History*, no. 28, p. 34.)

For each lesson you should make out a lesson plan along the lines of the one below. If you do not do it formally, you should have gone through the stages listed in your mind.

Lesson Plan

(tick in space if previously covered in long-term planning)

Date: Form: Room No.:

Course aims and objectives

Lesson objectives

Content

Techniques/teaching strategies

Resources

Planning-timing of lesson activities

Note on point reached by end of lesson/things you need to remember for next lesson

Evaluation of lesson

Follow-up

1 Discuss your long-term planning with your head of department.
2 Modify your strategic and tactical planning according to the circumstances you face.
3 At the end of the term write an evaluation of how valuable you have felt the planning to be.

**Focus 3
MANAGEMENT TECHNIQUES AND TEACHING SKILLS**

PART ONE   CLASS MANAGEMENT

What to do: Select a lesson when you are teaching history and you can arrange for a colleague to watch you at work. Get him or her to analyse your teaching, using the outline below in Section B. Before this, carry out the advice given in Section A.

Section A   Learning Names

Learning names is crucial.
For your first lesson:

... draw a plan of the desk layout in the classroom
... give each pupil a piece of paper with his/her seat number marked on it. Get the class to fill in their names
... collect the papers, and use them to make out a seating plan
... *insist* that they stick to those seats for a period from then on
... for each subsequent lesson try to learn the names of 3-4 pupils who sit near each other.

Section B   Managing Techniques

The essential element in all teaching is successful classroom management. It is of paramount importance to lay this down at your *first encounter* with a form. The picture you form in their minds will be with them throughout the course, and a poor beginning is hard to rectify. For each lesson establish a routine such as the one below.

1   Get to the classroom *before* the pupils. If you cannot:
    – Do *not* let them into the classroom, as this can produce a disorderly atmosphere hard to put right.
    – If you have to let them in and they are disorderly on arrival, throw them out and get them back in in a disciplined manner.

2   Lay out the work and prepare the classroom for teaching from the moment the pupils enter. This is easier at the start of the day, after breaks and lunch.

3   Have a clear *model* in your mind of the perfect teaching relationship or pattern that you want.

4   Lay down a set of explicit or implicit rules to achieve this. Make sure the class knows what the *rules* are.

5   Set *high* but realistic/optimistic/attainable goals.

6   Bear in mind the following check-list of things that *good* teachers do:

    ... plan the lesson properly
    ... know the pupils' names
    ... teach in an interesting manner
    ... use praise and humour constructively
    ... exercise full control over all aspects of the lesson.

7   Lay down a pattern to follow each lesson. This might include:

    ... crisp starting – pupils outside/inside/settle – routine of books/biros/pencils out, bags on floor
    ... start lesson in interesting manner/or settling down activity
    ... quick, efficient transition from one stage of lesson to the next
    ... give clear, explicit instructions
    ... make eye contact with as many pupils as possible in the lesson; make sure all pupils are paying attention; use frequent questions, stops, etc. to bring back into lesson those who are wandering around mentally
    ... continually reinforce rules laid down at start of the course
    ... follow twenty-minute rule – no activity to last longer than that

. . . give time to end lesson efficiently
. . . quick, efficient, disciplined exit from classroom.

Follow-up

1 Discuss with your fellow student or colleague the effectiveness of the lesson observed. To what extent do you agree or disagree?

2 How would you approach this lesson if you were to teach it again?

PART TWO   TEACHING SKILLS

What to do: In Part 1 of this Focus you concentrated on management skills. Here, the centre of attention shifts to specific teaching skills. Choose a lesson when a colleague is available to watch you at work. Ask him or her to use the observation schedule given in Topic 12 in Part 1 to watch your lesson. A summary of this is given below.

Observation schedule:

1 Lesson beginning
2 Transitions
3 Clarity of explanations, instructions
4 Question technique
5 Language level
6 Pace of lesson
7 Teaching modes used (whole class, group, individualised learning)
8 Variety of approach
9 Appropriateness of content, resources, etc.
10 Lesson ending.

(*A note to the observer:* Pay special attention to any *critical events* which take place during the lesson and which illustrate good or bad practice, used or missed opportunities. Keep a separate note of these.)

Follow-up

1 At the end of the lesson you, the teacher, should make your own summary of your performance, listing the strengths and weaknesses of the lesson.

2 Discuss both accounts with the observer.

3 Comment on:
points you agree about
disagreements
the interpretation of the critical events
things to bear in mind for future lessons.

4 For more information on managing skills read Wragg, E.C., 1981, *Class Management and Control*, Macmillan.

**Focus 4
DISCUSSION
LEADERSHIP SKILLS**

What to do: Teacher-class/group/pupil discussion is an essential element in all teaching, including history. The Bullock Report stressed the importance of talk in the classroom as an element in a strategy for language development across the curriculum. Discussion plays a leading part in teasing out historical evidence, telling the historical story, reaching conclusions and the imaginative act of historical reconstruction.

This Focus uses a discussion leadership rating scale to help raise awareness of discussion leadership skills.

1 Observe another teacher whose lesson is discussion-based. Use the schedule to spot those skills which are used and those which do not occur; and/or

2 tape record one of your own lessons. Use the schedule to examine your own skills.

Follow-up

1 Analyse the tape you have made or your record of the lesson.

2 Study:
Kerry, T., 1981, 'The teacher's talk' in C.R. Sutton, *Communicating in the Classroom*, Hodder and Stoughton.

3 In discussion the teacher plays a leading role, although the following discussion patterns should be encouraged and employed as normal teaching strategies:

>Teacher-Individual
>Teacher-Pairs or Small groups
>Teacher-Class
>Individual pupil-Individual pupil (pair work)
>Group discussion (interactive between 2 or more pupils)
>Class discussion (without teacher)

Look over the leadership schedule. How would the discussion itself, and the leadership required, vary according to each of the above circumstances?

A discussion leadership rating scale

The leader...	Well done	Attempted to	Not done
1 presented the problems for discussion clearly			
2 promoted respect between individuals in the group			
3 showed sensitivity to the feelings of individuals in the group			
4 created an atmosphere for the free expression of opinion			
5 established good relations between him or herself and the group members			
6 kept the discussion relevant			
7 found healthy outlets for emotional tensions			
8 encouraged understanding between group members			
9 protected individuals from unnecessary group pressure			
10 asked questions designed to promote a free response			
11 was aware of his or her own position as a group member			
12 made clear the purpose of the group's task			
13 allowed the group members to express criticisms			
14 allowed individuals to modify their opinions without losing face			
15 encouraged independence of thought			
16 encouraged open-mindedness			
17 helped individuals become more articulate			
18 made the group face 'issues'			
19 made group members responsible for their own views			
20 inspired confidence in group members about him or herself as leader			
21 allowed scope for the expression of minority opinions			
22 encouraged reasoned argument			
23 was a good listener			
24 provided an atmosphere free from assessment			
25 helped members accept various levels of ability among peers			
26 created a cohesive group atmosphere			
27 encouraged pooling of knowledge within the group			
28 provided information when called upon so to do			
29 suggested ways in which to follow up the discussion			
30 reflected group feelings accurately in summing up			

**Focus 5
TEACHER INTERACTION
WITH THE PUPILS**

What makes up successful history teaching? To find out, you need to analyse in detail what goes on in a lesson. So far we have looked at general categories of behaviour. The interaction schedule enables you to look at the crucial element in teaching — teacher/pupil interaction.

What to do:

1. Make sure that you understand the different categories in the schedule. For each minute of the lesson note the activity of the whole class, groups or individual pupils in it in relation to their interaction behaviour.

2. To do this place a tick in the appropriate box for the type of behaviour occurring for each minute of the lesson. When an activity happens write down the number in one of the boxes by the side of the appropriate minute.

3. After the lesson make a brief note on how successful you think it was. Then study the completed schedule. What light does it throw upon your judgement?

Categories for interaction analyses (Flanders)

Teacher talk	Indirect influence	1*	*Accepts feeling* accepts and clarifies the feeling tone of the students in a non-threatening manner. Feelings may be positive or negative. Predicting or recalling feelings are included.
		2*	*Praises or encourages* praises or encourages student action or behaviour. Jokes that release tension, not at the expense of another individual, nodding head or saying, 'um hum?' or 'go on' are included.
		3*	*Accepts or uses ideas of student* clarifying, building, or developing ideas suggested by a student. As a teacher brings more of his or her own ideas into play, shift to category five.
		4*	*Asks questions* asking a question about content or procedure with the intent that a student answer.
	Direct influence	5*	*Lecturing* giving facts or opinions about content or procedure: expressing his own ideas, asking rhetorical questions.
		6*	*Giving directions* directions, commands, or orders to which a student is expected to comply.
		7*	*Criticizing (or) justifying authority* statements intended to change student behaviour from non-acceptable to acceptable pattern; bawling someone out; stating why the teacher is doing what he is doing; extreme self-reference.
Student talk		8*	*Student talk-response* a student makes a predictable response to teacher. Teacher initiates the contact or solicits student statement and sets limits to what the student says.
		9*	*Student talk-initiation* talk by students which they initiate. Unpredictable statements in response to teacher. Shift from 8 to 9 as student introduces own ideas.
		10	*Silence or confusion* Pauses, short periods of silence and periods of confusion in which communication cannot be understood by the observer.

*There is NO scale implied by these numbers. Each number is classificatory, it designates a particular kind of communication event. To write these numbers down during observation is to enumerate, not to judge a position on a scale. N.B. Use ONE MINUTE INTERVALS.

FIAC lesson observation sheet for up to 30 minutes of classroom interaction

Class: Subject:
Date: Observer:
Lesson (1st, 2nd, etc.):

Tally across — put down the number of category

01																			
02																			
03																			
04																			
05																			
06																			
07																			
08																			
09																			
10																			
11																			
12																			
13																			
14																			
15																			
16																			
17																			
18																			
19																			
20																			
21																			
22																			
23																			
24																			
25																			
26																			
27																			
28																			
29																			
30																			

Follow-up

1 What patterns of teacher and pupil behaviour emerge from the Flanders grid you have compiled?
2 How can the teaching of history be conducted so as to provide more varied patterns?
3 What are the relative number of contributions by teacher and pupils? Is this a desirable balance? If not, why not? How could it be improved?

**Focus 6
HANDLING IDEAS AND CONCEPTS**

Topics 4 and 7 in Part 1 introduced the ideas of teaching for concepts and the development of pupils' historical thinking. Historical thinking involves the handling of ideas and concepts. How you present them will influence the development of students' historical understanding.

What to do:

1 Read through Topics 4 and 7 in Part 1 and your previous work in those areas.
2 Choose a class in which concepts and ideas are being introduced.
3 Use the headings in Section A below to make detailed notes in the lesson on the way concepts and ideas were introduced and developed in the lesson. (Definitions of the concepts labelled in Section A are given in Section B.)

Section A   Class Observation

Class: Subject:
Date: Period:
Class Organisation (banded/mixed ability/streamed etc.):

Standard:

Concepts and ideas introduced or handled in the lesson (a full listing):

structural concepts

organisational concepts

specific concepts

simile and metaphor

giving examples

use of evidence

reinforcing the concept or idea

Section B   Concept Definitions and Notes on Observation Headings

Structural   Structural concepts are fundamental to the nature of the historical discipline. They deal with ideas such as cause, consequence, similarity, difference, change, continuity.

Organisational   Organisational concepts such as nationalism, feudalism or the word Norman (as used in the 'Norman Age') should relate to a background web of supporting ideas and information. Think of one *organisational concept* used in the lesson. How well was it related to the body of knowledge which the pupil knew or could comprehend? Was it tied implicitly or explicitly into this *extended context*? For example: was Norman linked to specifics such as: Normandy, Vikings, William the Conqueror, feudal system, barons, knights?

Specific (words)   History uses words which derive their *historical meaning* from the specific context in which they are used. For example, 'king' meant something very different in AD 800, 1200, 1600 and 1900, and in different countries and societies. How well was the specific meaning of such words explained in their historical context during the lesson? How did the teacher cope with problems of possible confusion in the use of terminology which has a radically different meaning today from the period in which it was being used?

The use of similes and metaphors   Every analogy is imperfect. For example, to explain what a Norman castle was like is a difficult task. The general concept of forts and castles is something which has to be developed through the use of analogy. For example, the teacher may say, 'A motte and bailey castle was like . . .'. How were similes and metaphors used to explain the concepts and ideas being observed?

45

Giving examples An area of simile and metaphor is the everyday experience of the pupils. For example, in dealing with the Norman warrior, the pupil can relate his weapons and armour to those of a modern soldier. Also, the role of the Norman knight can be compared to present-day troops operating in Northern Ireland or Germany. Such comparisons can heighten the pupils' understanding of the historical situation, while at the same time developing the *structural concepts* of change, continuity, contrast, similarity, cause, consequence and uniqueness.

Use of evidence What concrete use of evidence was there to reinforce the idea or concept with specific examples? How did the teacher deploy the resources available to build up the pupils' understanding?

Reinforcing the concept or idea How did the pupil tasks relate to reinforcing the idea or concept — i.e. what were the pupils asked to do to make sure that they had grasped the concept at their particular level?

Follow-up

Read Rogers, P.J., 1979, chapter IV, 2, *Concept, procedure and narrative* and then use the structure he presents to analyse *in detail* how you have developed one concept with your pupils.

Focus 7
QUESTIONS IN THE CLASSROOM

The asking of questions is the pivot around which history teaching revolves. The understanding of any historical situation depends upon a study of evidence, either of a primary or secondary kind. 'Every step in the argument depends on asking a question. The question is the charge of gas, exploded in the cylinder-head, which is the motive force of every piston-stroke. But the metaphor is not adequate, because each new piston-stroke is produced not by exploding another charge of the same old mixture but by exploding a charge of a new kind.' (Collingwood, R.G., 1946, *The Idea of History*, Oxford University Press, p. 273.) The nature of classroom questioning is therefore crucial to the teaching of history. Questions are of many kinds. The table in Section A suggests some of the ways in which teachers use them.

What to do: *Either* observe a lesson taught by another teacher *or* tape-record one of your own. Analyse the questions according to the types described in Section A opposite; record your findings on a grid like the one in Section B.

Section A Types of Question

Question type	Explanation
1 A *data recall* question	requires the pupil to remember facts without putting them to any use. E.g. 'When was the Battle of Hastings?'
2 A *naming* question	asks the pupil to *name* something without showing how it relates to the historical situation. E.g. 'What are the men in the picture wearing?'
3 An *observation* question	asks pupils to describe something without relating it to their knowledge of the situation. E.g. 'Describe what is happening in the picture.'
4 A *reasoning* question	asks the pupils to explain something. E.g. 'What does the picture tell us about how the Normans and Saxons fought?'
5 A *speculative* question	the pupil is asked to consider how the situation might have developed, or what led up to it. E.g. 'What do you think happened next?'
6 An *empathetic* question	asks the pupil to become involved personally with the evidence. E.g. 'If you had been the soldier standing behind Harold, say what you might have thought, felt and done at the moment the arrow hit him in the eye.'
7 A *hypothesis generating* question	asks the pupils to speculate about possible causes and consequences. E.g. 'What factors led Harold to fight the battle at that place and time?'
8 A *problem solving* question	one which asks the pupils to weigh up the evidence. 'What evidence does the picture contain that Harold was shot in the eye?'
9 An *evidence questioning* question	questions that look at the veracity of the evidence. E.g. 'On what do you think the weavers of the tapestry based their picture?' 'How reliable is the tapestry as evidence about the battle?'
10 A *synthesising* question	a question that pulls the questioning process together, and allows for a resolution of the problem. E.g. 'Write an account of the Battle of Hastings from the viewpoint of *either* Bishop Odo *or* Harold's standard bearer.'
11 A *control* question	relates to getting pupils to behave, rather than their learning. E.g. 'Will you shut up, Joan?'
12 A *closed* question	questions of 'guess the teachers' mind' variety, which often appear to be open-ended. E.g. 'What happened to Harold at Hastings?' (a traditional teacher that is.)

Section B Observing a Lesson

Use the schedule below to analyse the questions in a lesson you observe.

Class: Subject:
Date: Lesson:
Nature of lesson (content, pattern of teaching, etc.)
Class organisation (banded/mixed ability/streamed/level)
Place a tick in the appropriate box when a particular type of question is asked.

		0	5	10	15	20	25	30	35	40	45
1	Data recall										
2	Naming										
3	Observation										
4	Reasoning										
5	Speculative										
6	Empathetic										
7	Hypothesis generating										
8	Problem solving										
9	Evidence questioning										
10	Synthesising										
11	Control										
12	Closed										

(minutes)

Follow-up

1. From your observation, work out the sequence in which the questioning was used to resolve the historical problem the class faced. Was there a move from low order to higher order questioning? Was the questioning successful? How would you have improved it?

2. If possible get a fellow teacher or student to observe your own teaching. Ask him or her to use the observation schedule in Section B, and also to make out a seating plan for the form. On the seating plan get your observer to tick a pupil's place every time you ask that pupil a question. At the end of the lesson discuss the nature of your questioning, and how many pupils you involved in the lesson.

3. Read Unwin, R., 1981, *Visual Dimension in the Study and Teaching of History*, Historical Association, TH49. This is an excellent introduction to the use of questioning related to visual evidence.

4. On the skills of questioning read Kerry, T., 1982, *Effective Questioning*, Macmillan, *Focus* books.

**Focus 8
INDIVIDUAL PUPILS
AT WORK**

Teaching should be an enjoyable profession, in which teachers and pupils participate together in the learning process. Successful teaching depends upon motivating and retaining the interest and enthusiasm of the pupils. How can you tell if a teacher is relating successfully to individual pupils? Detailed observation can help. The following activities will help you focus in on pupils working in different ways.

What to do:

1. Choose a lesson in which you think there will be a range of activities.
2. Before the lesson work out how to operate the observation schedule. Make sure that you have been with the class on several occasions, so that you know them and they know you. Consult the teacher about one pupil you would like to observe. Choose a child who *participates fully and constructively* in the lessons. Do *not* let the child know that you are going to watch him or her.
3. During the lesson. At the end of each minute, tick what the child did for that minute. You may have up to three ticks for any one minute. If you are watching a double period, use two colours for your ticks, and on the 36th minute start again at 1. Begin ticking the schedule when the teaching starts, and the pupils are involved in learning.
4. After the lesson. Without letting the pupil know that you have been observing him or her, talk to him or her about the lesson and record the pupil's impressions.
5. Analyse your observations as follows:
   — count each tick as one minute if there is only one tick in that minute.
   — otherwise count as ½ or ⅓ of a minute, according to the number of ticks.
   — add up the amount of time the pupil has spent on each activity and enter the total.
   — work out what each time total represents as a proportion of the lesson.

Follow-up

1. Discuss your observation, notes on the pupil and lesson analysis with a colleague or fellow student.
2. How would you have planned out a more fruitful use of pupil 'on-task' activity? How would you have avoided 'off-task' behaviour during the lesson?
3. Carry out the same observation for a *non-participating* pupil. How would you have improved his or her participation in the lesson?

PUPIL OBSERVATION

Class: Subject:

Activity	1	2	3	4	5	6	7	8	9	10	11	12	13	14	15	16	17	18	19	20	21	22	23	24	25	26	27	28	29	30	31	32	33	34	35	Total time	%
Listening																																					
Observing																																					
Discuss with teacher																																					
Discuss with pupil(s)																																					
Practical																																					
Deliberating																																					
Not involved																																					
Reading Book																																					
Worksheet																																					
Blackboard																																					
Exercise book																																					
Other																																					
Writing Copying																																					
Answering questions																																					
Recording																																					
Other																																					
Self-initiated																																					

BRIEF SUMMARY OF LESSON
Time in minutes   Class activity   PUPIL RESPONSE

**Focus 9
TEACHING SLOW
LEARNERS**

History classes often cover the whole of the ability range, particularly in the first year of secondary schooling and in the junior and middle schools. As a history teacher you will spend a lot of your time with slow learners. In a streamed or banded situation the lower streams or bands will be predominantly made up of slow learners. You will need a positive approach to their teaching. This should be coupled to a conscious effort to circumvent the inferior status which these youngsters may have been given.

What to do: Read the preamble material in Section A below to start you thinking about the problems of the slower learner.

Then study slow learners using the outlines provided by Section B. Finally, complete the follow-up activities.

Section A

Two facts are clear:
1 there are substantial numbers of slow learners in secondary schools. 14 per cent was the conservative estimate of a DES survey, with a range from 7 to 60 per cent in a representative sample of schools.
2 not all teachers can spot the slow learners. Movement from class to class in a large secondary school makes identification difficult for teachers and many pupils who seem slow in other ways are adept at covering up their shortcomings. They drift from lesson to lesson, with little help from teaching staff.

Who are the slow learners? A simple definition is that they are children who are failing in the school work given to the whole ability range. They give the impression that they may need special help over a lengthy period, and their record shows that they have been unable to cope for a long time.

'Slow learners' is a synonym for older terms like: backward, thick, less able, educationally subnormal and remedial.

An added complication is that since the Warnock Report there has been a move to integrate handicapped and educationally subnormal children into normal schools. Previously they were educated in separate establishments.

Slow learners are only *one sub-group* of a number of children with learning difficulties. The school department which deals with such groups (often the remedial department) contains groups of children who may fall into one or several of these categories:

. . . slow learners
. . . children with specific learning difficulties
. . . children with physical handicaps
. . . behaviour problems
. . . social, cultural and/or ethnic disadvantages.

To teach slow learners you must first identify their specific needs, and then plan a course of action. The course of action should involve specific teaching materials, record keeping and evaluation.

Section B

1 First, try to be positive. Think of four ways in which slowness is a *desirable* characteristic.

2 Try to identify the problems of an individual slow learner. Think of a child who seems unable to cope with the history lesson. Write down as many observations as you can about the problems he or she seems to be encountering. These can take the form of:
 — has difficulty in reading, writing
 — makes mistakes copying
 — needs a lot of face-to-face help
 — writes in short, incomplete sentences
 — uncoordinated
 — writes messy disorganised work

Then by the side of each comment write down the category or classification under which that disability falls, from this list: intellectual, academic performance, physical, social, emotional.

3 Observe a class with slow learners in it, using the following schedule:

Class: Subject:
Date: Lesson:
Class organisation (banded/streamed/mixed ability etc.)

Nature of pupils' problems, for specific teaching:

Tasks devised to assist with this:

Pupils' relationships with peers and teacher:

Evaluation of the success of teaching strategy:

4 Prepare materials to teach the same pupils for their next lesson, with a rationale. Think of: language level, interest, suitability of tasks, understandability of visual material used.

Follow-up

1 It might be useful to consult the following:

   M. Wilson, 1982, 'Teaching history to slow learners, problems of language and communication', *Teaching History*, No. 33.

   M. Wilson, 1982, 'The attitudes of slow-learning adolescents to the teaching and study of history', *Teaching History*, No. 34.

   J. Hull, 1978, 'Practical points on teaching history to less-able secondary pupils', *Teaching History*, No. 28.

2 Use your department's publishers' catalogues to order samples of the following materials for slow learners. Then put them into the order of suitability for your own slow learners.

   Flashback, Hutchinson
   Action history, Edward Arnold
   Exploring history, Oliver and Boyd
   Wide range history, Oliver and Boyd
   Time traveller, Usborne
   History workshop, Cassell
   Headline history, Evans

3 For more information on this theme consult Kerry, T. and Bell, P., 1982, *Teaching Slow Learners*, Macmillan, *Focus* series.

**Focus 10
TEACHING QUICK LEARNERS**

At the other end of the spectrum from the slow learners there is the problem of handling quick learners. This is particularly acute in mixed ability classes, or where there is a wide range of ability in a form. At one extreme the problem of the quick learner means that some pupils will be demonstrably cleverer than you are — they have better memories, livelier imaginations and can think more clearly. Teaching quick learners means that you have to produce resources and teaching ideas to stretch them, and to enable them to participate fully in lessons. If you do not, the danger is that they will underachieve and even become disruptive.

What to do: Read Section A below to start you thinking. Then, use the schedule in Section B to make a close study of two or three bright pupils during a typical lesson. Finally, complete the follow-up activities to this Focus.

Section A

There are three elements in teaching quick learners — identification/diagnosis; teaching; and evaluation. Identification is more difficult than it might seem, for often quick learners either disguise their ability, or show their ability in a non-formal manner — such as in their verbal responses. Verbal acuity may not be represented in written responses — the pupil may even be functionally illiterate. Other problems relate to physical and neurological problems, and to the simple fact that the teaching may be uninspired and not require pupil responses which enable the identification of quickness. The teaching of quick learners demands an imaginative response from the teacher to produce appropriate tasks. Evaluation is crucial, for it not only allows diagnosis, but enables you to see if your teaching is being effective.

Section B

Class: Subject:
Date:
Nature of lesson
Class organisation (banded/mixed ability/streamed etc.)

Ways in which teacher stretches the bright pupils

Relationship of special activities or work set to the main teaching pattern or theme of the lesson

Pupils' performance during their activities

Nature of learning achieved by pupils

Pupil relationships with peers and teacher

Follow-up

1   Discuss the lesson with the teacher, with particular emphasis upon the quick learners.

2   Ask a fellow student or colleague to observe one of your lessons, with particular attention to the work of the quick learners.

3   Keep a record of your teaching of bright pupils over half a term. Concentrate on questions of: general strategy, provision of teaching approaches and materials, assessment. At the end of this, say how successful you think you were, and how you adapted your teaching to changing circumstances.

4   Some ideas for the evaluation of work by quick learners can be gleaned from Dickinson, A.K. and Lee, P.J. (eds), 1978, chapters 5 and 6, where they discuss their analysis of children's levels of thinking in relation to their testing. For a more general review of the problems of bright pupils in normal schools you may care to read Kerry, T. (ed.), 1983, *Finding and Helping the Able Child,* Croom Helm.

Focus 11
GROUP WORK

Group work is an important element in history teaching. Group work means that pupils can cooperate in their learning, and benefit both educationally and socially from the group activity. Group activity can take many forms, and with the development of classroom drama and associated small group activities in gaming and simulation it is of increasing importance. To the teacher it has the advantage of allowing a *different form of classroom activity* from the stereotype of teacher-pupil/class interaction.

What to do: Choose a lesson where the pupils are divided up into working groups; for example when they are doing group projects, preparing a play, etc. Observe the lesson. In your observation concentrate on the nature of the group activity.

Using the outline provided, describe the ways in which the groups were handled by the teacher, the tasks which they were engaged in, and the specific values of group work as opposed to other forms of lesson organisation.

Class: Subject:
Nature of lesson:

Class organisation (banded/mixed ability/streamed etc.)

Standard:

Nature of grouping of pupils (numbers in each group, sex)

On what criteria were the pupils grouped together?

Describe the group's tasks

Assess the success of each activity in progress

Moving around Plot the groups on a classroom plan. For ten minutes track the teacher's movements between groups. (If you are being observed by a colleague or fellow student, he or she does this.) Indicate how long is spent with each group. Try also to note the vigilance with which other groups' activities are observed.

Follow-up

1. Assess how successful you think the lesson was.
2. Consider how the classroom *atmosphere* differed from a traditional lesson.
3. Plan out how you would introduce group work into your own lessons during the coming week. What advantages do you think such activities might have over those you had previously planned?
4. What special skills does a teacher need to handle this form of organisation?
5. Are there special skills required in task-setting for groups?
6. To explore this topic in more detail, consult
   Kerry, T. and Sands, M.K., 1982, *Handling Classroom Groups*, Macmillan, *Focus* series.

Part 3   REFLECTIONS ON EXPERIENCE

This part of the book aims to give you the opportunity to reflect upon some of the lessons you have learned from your observation and teaching experiences. The elements contained in it are not intended to be catholic, but should spotlight different features of the teaching landscape. Topic A extends the examination of history teaching and language across the curriculum. It concentrates on pupil talk, writing and textbook language. Topic B raises the crucial issues of assessment — the keystone of successful teaching — and suggests possible ways of producing a profile for written work. In Topic C the searchlight picks up a completely different aspect of the terrain, the development of several new teaching approaches. This list is not comprehensive, and reflects a wide variety of innovation in history teaching in the past decade. At the other end of the teaching spectrum is the question of examining — Topic D. The thrust of Topic D is how to cope with the realities of the examination system which dominates so much teaching in the 14-16 age range. Topic E concentrates on the history department, and suggests how you might evaluate its work. It is hoped that these five sections of Part 3 will help heighten awareness, and, if somewhat eclectic, will be both stimulating and suggestive. The book ends with a reading list.

Topic A
HISTORY TEACHING AND LANGUAGE ACROSS THE CURRICULUM

The school plays a key role in developing each pupil's English language skills. The history department should play a big part in your school's language policy. Indeed, language development should be at the heart of your history teaching if you accept that history is as much a *procedural* subject as one concerned with propositional knowledge (see Part 1, Topic 5). In your history teaching you should consider what forms of communication you are using and fostering. How important do you consider the following, and how often do you employ them in your teaching?

(a) Pupil talk, either in pairs or small groups to discuss or resolve problems.
(b) Pupil reporting to the class, either singly or in groups.
(c) Writing in a rough, unstructured form to allow for the loose formulation of ideas and the development of open-ended thinking.
(d) Writing of a highly imaginative, subjective form which has the *pupil* as an audience instead of the teacher. In this writing the pupil is writing for him or herself.
(e) Drawing, as a way of showing what a pupil *understands* about a topic, instead of copying a picture.
(f) The kind of language you use and which is used in textbooks. Is it appropriate? How does it fit into the pupil's own linguistic framework?

The acquisition and development of vocabulary is integral to history teaching. It is a major thread running through the fabric of your teaching. The examples below relate to the teaching of World History, but the underlying principles apply to all history teaching. Simple words, as in 'A' below, have historical antecedents. The *structural* and *specific* concepts (see Focus 4) in 'B' largely derive their meaning from their historical context. The words in 'C' are taken from a selection of CSE and 'O' level World History textbooks. The vocabulary illustrates the sophistication of vocabulary which history fosters, and which is an integral element in developing historical understanding. The list was originally produced to show the incomprehensibility of such textbooks, but a more optimistic interpretation is possible.

LANGUAGE AND WORLD HISTORY

A Normal language (loan words)

'Returning to the *bungalow* through the *jungle* she threw her *calico* bonnet on the *teak* table, put on her *gingham* apron and slipped into a pair of *sandals*. There was the *tea-caddy* to fill, the *chutney* to prepare for the *curry*, *pepper* and *cheroots* to order from the *bazaar* – she would send a *chit*. The children were out in the *dinghy* and their *khaki dungarees* were sure to be wet. She needed *shampoo*, she still had to mend Tom's *pyjamas* and she never had finished those *chintz* hangings for the *veranda*. Ah well! she really didn't give a *damn* and putting a *shawl* round her shoulders she poured herself some *punch*.'

B Structural and Specific Concepts

Government	Environment
Industrialisation	Agriculture
Migration	Cultural Diffusion
Imperialism and Nationalism	Conflict
Women's changing role	Social Stratification
Communications	Religion
Science	Technology
Urbanisation	

C Historical vocabulary

Absolution	Disturbance	Pacifism
Aggression	Dominion	Parliament
Ally	Dynasty	Partisan
Amnesty	Economics	Partition
Anarchism	Election	Plebiscite
Annex	Elite	Politics
Armistice	Empire	President
Arms Race	Equality	Prime Minister
Assassination	Ethnic	Propaganda-indoctrination
Asylum	Fascism	Provisional Government
Autocracy	Federation	Racism
Automation	Foreign Aid	Radical
Balance of Power	Foreign Policy	Rationing
Ballistic Missile	Franchise	Reactionary
Blockade-Embargo	Freedom of Speech	Rebellion
Border	Frontier	Referendum
Bureaucracy	Genocide	Reform
Cabinet	Government	Refugee
Capitalism	Guerilla	Regime
Caste	Ideology	Representative
Censorship	Imperialism	Republic
Centralisation	Independence	Resolution
Civil Disobedience	Industrialisation	Revolt
Civil Liberties	Isolationism	Revolution
Civil Rights	Insurrection	Riot
Civil War	Invasion	Sanctuary
Class	Judicial Review	Sanctions
Coalition	Junta	Satellite
Colonialism	Justification	Sect
Collaboration	Kingdom	Secular
Collective	Legislation	Senate
Collective Security	Liberalism	Separation of Powers
Communism	Liberate	Socialism
Community	Mandate	Sovereignty
Congress	Marxism { Leninism / Stalinism / Bolshevism }	State
Conscription		Strategy
Consensus		Strike
Conservation	Mass Media	Suffrage
Constitution	Mediation	Summit
Council	Migration	Super-power
Coup d'état	Military Base	Tactics
Decolonisation	Military – Militarism	Technology
Declaration	Minister	Territory
Demagogue	Minority	Terrorist
Democracy	Mobilisation	The Left
Demonstration	Mobilise	The Right
Depression	Monarch	The West
Deterrent	Nation	Totalitarianism
Developing	Nationalisation	Treaty
Dictator	Nationalism	Tribalism
Delegate	Neutrality	Union
Diplomacy	Nuclear	Urbanisation
Discrimination	Occupation	Veto
	Oligarchy	
	Opposition	

Activity 14:
Looking at language in history lessons

Examine the work of two classes you have taught from the viewpoint of language development. From each class take a sample of three pupils' work — the most able, the average and the least able. Also consult your teaching records and the resources you used, for example textbooks, workcards and audio-visual aids.

This Activity aims to analyse how you developed linguistic skills in the individual pupils scrutinised.

Class 1 (brief notes)

Pupil 1 What new words did you introduce to the pupil?

How did you encourage him or her to understand these?

In what ways did you attempt to improve his or her range of linguistic skills?

Pupil 2 New words:

Encouragement of understanding:

Fostering of linguistic skills:

Pupil 3 New words:

Encouragement of understanding:

Fostering of linguistic skills:

Class 2
(Follow the same procedure as for Class 1.)

Follow-up
Levine, N., 1981, (see 'Further Reading' on p. 71) is an excellent introduction to the question of language and history teaching. Marland, M. (ed.), 1977, *Language Across the Curriculum,* contains many interesting ideas. He looks closely at the idea of pupils using language in different ways. These ideas are more fully formulated in Martin, N. et al., 1976, *Writing and Learning Across the Curriculum.* A.D. Edwards examines the concept of 'register' — the way in which pupils and teachers use language according to their circumstances — in 'The "Language of History" and the Communication of Historical Knowledge' in Dickinson, A.K. and Lee, P.J. (eds), 1978. Use these references to further your own study of this topic.

**Topic B
PUPIL ASSESSMENT**

The assessment of pupil progress is an essential element in the work of a teacher. Not only does it help develop pupils' historical understanding, but is also an invaluable check on the success of the teaching. Detailed recording in the form suggested below may be impossible, as many history teachers see from 300 to 350 pupils a week. However, the technique can be used for sampling or for checking on specific pupil progress, or the lack of it.

Every teacher has a mark book. What should it contain for each form you teach?

1. A full list of pupils' names — forenames and surnames, dates of birth, details of house or tutor group.
2. Seating plan — initially to record names.
3. Key page — for recording details of work set and the criteria for assessing pupil performance.
4. Record page — with results for all the class on one double page, using the key page.
5. Individual pupil record details — to record details of individual pupil progress.

Your records should enable you to build up a profile of your pupils and their learning progress. Each piece of work can be assessed on five linked points — presentation, effort, language level, thinking level and imagination — PELTI for short.

The Key page

Refer to these profile elements when evaluating work. The numbers refer to the record page.

1. *Presentation* — five-point scale of your own devising, a-e (e.g. very neat, neat, . . .)
2. *Effort* — five-point scale of your own devising, a-e (e.g. very hard work, hard work, . . .)
3. *Language level* — five-point scale, a-e, as follows:
   (a) sophisticated use of English. Paragraphs in homogenous units, with an argument running through the whole piece of work.
   (b) clear, accurate use of English. Well structured paragraphs. Grammatically accurate. Language unsophisticated.
   (c) writing clear. Paragraphs develop simple idea or ideas. Sentences show incomplete grasp of grammar. Language at a concrete, descriptive level.
   (d) limited in volume. Lacks clarity. Work incomplete in relation to task set. Unsound grammar and spelling. Poor sentence structure.
   (e) writing confused and incomplete. Non-grammatical sentences. Spelling weak. Very simple vocabulary.
4. *Thinking level* — use a five-point scale a-e as follows:
   (a) Able to handle a range of sources and evidence, and imaginatively to reconstruct historical situation or to provide a sophisticated explanation of it.
   (b) Able to cross-refer between sources, and to understand the historical situation. Thinking reveals a grasp of the historical context.
   (c) Able to make simple generalisations on the basis of evidence, and to cross-refer between sources. Explanations related to the immediately observable evidence.
   (d) Conclusions drawn from one or two sources. Ideas at a very simple, concrete level of explanation.
   (e) Little understanding shown. Only able to comprehend single pieces of evidence.
5. *Imagination/empathy* — five-point scale of your own devising, a-e.

Below or opposite the profile elements, list details of the work set.

The *key page* allows you to set out a *record page* with a record of the whole form's progress, and *individual pupil record details*. The *individual pupil record* should contain any information you have discovered about the pupil, e.g. Verbal Reasoning Quotient, any disabilities, personality traits. The layout of records is as follows:

Record page entries
M = Mark   D = Done
Work Set = initial at side

PUPIL'S NAME:

	P	E	L	T	I	M	D		P	E	L	T	I	M	D
a								b							
c								d							
e								f							

Individual pupil record details

Pupil's name: Date of birth:
Comments

Activity 15: Record Keeping

1. Make out your own *key page*.
2. Take a sample of exercise books from two forms you teach. The sample should consist of one very good book, one average and one poor for each form.
3. Assess your pupils' work using the key page. Then consider how valuable you consider the exercise, and what you have learnt from it about your pupils and your own teaching.
4. Every book you mark should contain some *constructive comments*. Read through the marking you have done for your forms, and consider whether you have been helpful, and whether you could have marked in a more positive and productive manner.

Follow-up

Assessment is a major area of concern. An introduction to the issues involved is contained in Macintosh, H.G., 1976, *Assessment and the Secondary School Teacher*, Routledge & Kegan Paul.

Consider how you might apply the skills and objectives outlined in Coltham, J.B. and Fines, J., 1971, to the evaluation of your own pupils' work. How valuable is the taxonomic approach?

**Topic C
INNOVATIONS IN HISTORY TEACHING**

History teaching is in a state of flux. Traditional approaches are being fused with newer classroom practices. Although the new wine is bursting a few of the older bottles, on the whole there is a palatable mixture. Five innovations of the past decade are:

(a) Drama in history
(b) Family history
(c) Games and simulations
(d) Schools Council history project
(e) Computing.

There have also been significant changes in approaches to assessment and examining.

During your last term of teaching, what innovations did you attempt, or were associated with in your department's work? What was your best teaching idea? If you were unable to be innovative, what would you have liked to have done?

Activity 16: Experimenting with teaching methods

Complete the activities below, and then talk about them with your colleagues or fellow students, including your best teaching idea.

Innovations during teaching

Below each heading make a comment about when you used that method, and how the lesson went:

Drama in history

Family history

Games and simulations

Schools Council history project

Computing

My best teaching idea

Class: Subject:
Date:

Nature of lesson

Class organisation

Teaching idea/lesson plan

Evaluation of lesson — how did it go? Why?

Innovations I would have liked

Write a report on innovations you would have liked to have seen in your own teaching, and in the department. Be specific about *how* you would have introduced the ideas.

Follow-up

Information upon the innovations mentioned is contained in the following:

DRAMA IN HISTORY   Fines, J. and Verrier, R., 1974, *The drama of history*, New University Education.

FAMILY HISTORY   Steel, D. and Taylor, L., 1973, *Family history in schools*, Phillimore.
GAMES AND SIMULATIONS   Birt, D. and Nichol, J., 1975, *Games and simulations in history*, Longman.
SCHOOLS COUNCIL HISTORY PROJECT   Schools Council Project History 13-16, 1976, *What is history?*, Holmes McDougall.
COMPUTING   *Teaching History* vol. 33, June 1982, contains a number of articles on the subject. Nichol, J. and Dean, J. (eds), *History Teaching and Computing*, Basil Blackwell, in preparation, will develop ideas about history teaching and computing.

**Topic D
EXAMINATION WORK**

This section is in two parts. First, there is a list of recommended stages you need to go through in order to prepare yourself for examination work. Second, there is an Activity which helps you plan your teaching for examination classes. Such preparation is essential, and should be part of general departmental policy.

1   Obtain a copy of the syllabus, and the *sections of it* which the department covers.
2   Send for copies of the *last five years'* examination papers.
(a)   Familiarise yourself with the types of questions asked, and their relative proportions, i.e. essay, short answer, multiple choice, etc.
(b)   For the sections of the syllabus which the department teaches, analyse the questions asked under a grid for each year, and for the topics which they cover.
   The old examination papers are your REAL syllabus and will tell you exactly what you will teach in terms of content.
3   Obtain copies of departmental notes/worksheets/workbooks etc., and the textbook(s) which it uses as the core for its teaching.
4   Try to observe as many examination lessons as you can; either by your colleagues, or, if you are a student, on your visit to the school, to sort out your teaching programme. It is very important to conform *in general* to departmental teaching style. To break away with a radically different approach can result in chaos.
5   Obtain as full a breakdown of the ability range of pupils as you can. Find out what is the range. Mixed CSE/'O' level forms have a very wide range indeed, *as can 'A' level forms*, i.e. from 'O' level failures to university scholarship standard.
6   Provide a handout for the pupils of the syllabus and general organisation of the teaching you propose.
7   *Teaching*   How you teach towards exams is very much a personal question, and you will need to work out your own style. Try to mark regularly and quickly – i.e. as soon as work is handed in. There is no great pupil enthusiasm to hand in examination type essays, and punctual marking encourages punctual writing. After each essay, it is a good idea to work out on the board the points which should have been covered, and possible interpretations of the question.
8   *Exam preparation*   Writing exam answers is an acquired skill, and needs lots of practice. Because of shortage of time towards the end of the course, see if you can hold timed essays in the lunch hour, or free periods. Organise your lunch-time essay-writing before other departments do!

Short factual tests on specific elements in the course are useful for building up the body of knowledge which conventional exam sitting requires.

Make sure that the pupils have seen and worked on a range of the old papers. Thus they will be familiar with what is involved when they enter the examination room.

**Activity 17:
Planning examination work**

Find out which examination syllabus (CSE and/or GCE) applies to the school in which you are working. Also, *obtain a copy* of the appropriate examination regulations. *Break down* your syllabus into a series of topics to be studied on a year-planner of the kind shown below. Remember to leave a margin of error for interruptions (e.g. choir practice, sports days) and to allow appropriate periods for revision to practise exam techniques.

TERM 1 Week 1

              2

              3

              4

              5 etc.

Repeat the process for Terms 2 and 3, and year 2 if necessary.

Topic E
HOW TO EVALUATE A HISTORY DEPARTMENT

At the end of your study period, complete the following questionnaire. It also makes for excellent reading before being interviewed for a (new) job! The questionnaire, written by John Highham, is titled 'How to evaluate a history department' and comes from *Teaching History*, June 1979, No. 24, pp. 14-15.

Activity 18:
The Questionnaire

1 *Yourself (and the other teachers)*
How many history books have you read this year
— for your teaching?
— for interest?
How many historical novels have you read?
How many books about teaching have you read?
Have you had regular contact with
— an historical or archaeological society?
— an association of history teachers?
— a teachers' association?
How many lectures/conferences/courses have you attended this year?
Do you regularly read
— *History/History Today/Teaching History*?
— the *Times Educational Supplement*?
— any other professional journal?
How often have you visited, during the year
— a record office?
— a museum of national importance?
— a museum of local importance?
— a specialist library?
— your local teachers' centre?
— your local college/university?
— new historical sites/buildings?
— special exhibitions?
Do you regularly undertake personal research
— of an historical nature?
— of an educational nature?
How regularly do you co-operate with other history teachers
— in your own school?
— in your area?

2 *Your teaching (and that of other teachers)*
Is the quality of your teaching improving year by year?
How thoroughly do you plan your lessons?
Do you regularly and effectively use the following aids
— a tape recorder?

— slide/film strip projector?
— overhead projector?
— 16 mm film projector?
— TV videotape?

Do you regularly use or experiment with the following approaches to your work?
— documents?
— other source material?
— local history?
— fieldwork?
— worksheets?
— individual/group projects?
— lecturettes?
— role playing/mock trials/discussions?
— plays/other imaginative work?
— games or simulations?
— model making?

Do you constantly strive for variety of approach?
How often do you teach a subject which is new to you?
Do you study how your colleagues teach?
Have you tried team-teaching?
Do you help to run a history or model making club?
Do you help with excursions/field trips

3 *The pupils*

How many of your pupils continue the study of history after they can drop it?
How does this compare with the school/county/national average?
Do any pupils opt for history as the 'lesser evil'?
Do any regret having opted for it?
How many in your classes think history irrelevant or boring?
Does history become a 'middle class subject' by the fifth year?
How many GCE pupils actively enjoy history lessons?
How many CSE pupils actively enjoy history lessons?
How many non-exam pupils actively enjoy history lessons?
Do you bring in sixth-formers to help with group work with younger and less able pupils?
How many non-literary ways have you tried with your weakest classes?
How often do your more able pupils discuss/report on books they have read, in groups?
Do you teach your pupils to use reference books and libraries efficiently?
Have they access to school libraries and history rooms at lunchtimes?
How many ask for history readers to take home?
How many regularly read historical novels?
How many opt to continue their historical studies in the sixth form
— for 'A' level?
— for other exams?
— for enjoyment?

How many complain if they are unable to continue with history in the sixth form?
What contacts have your sixth-formers had with college/university history departments?
How many opt to read for a degree in history?
How many opt to specialise in history at training college?
How many pupils participate in voluntary history
— in school societies?
— in the Historical Association?
— in fieldwork?
— in excursions/courses?
— model making?

Does each child get to his correct destination?
What would your pupils write on your end of term report?

4 *Assessment*

Do you regularly set, check and mark homework?
Can your weaker pupils do supervised private study instead?
Is your marking up to date?
Is it positive rather than negative?
Do you praise rather than blame?
Do you adapt your standard of marking to encourage or shock as appropriate?
Do you correct spelling, grammar and style?
Are your marginal comments constructive?
Do you regularly write a general comment at the end of a completed piece of work?
Do you regularly test facts and understanding?
How much variety do you put into your method of testing?
How do you reward an exceptional piece of work?
Do your exams test effectively what has been taught, skills as well as knowledge?
Do your pupils enjoy their exams?
Do you make exams an aid to learning?
How do you record each child's
— ability?
— attainment?
— interest?
— effort?
— attitude?
— progress?
How does the department correlate and co-ordinate this?
Who is consulted before a child is placed in a set or transferred to a new one?
Do you give full, frank, fair and detailed testimonials/references if asked?

5 *The classroom and specialist rooms*

Is it obvious that the classrooms in which you teach are used for history?
Are the wall displays relevant to your teaching?
Is there a time chart
— of the whole span of history?
— of the year's work in history?
Is there teacher's work and pupils' work on display as well as bought items?
Are the wall displays changed regularly?
Do the pupils help in the selection and arrangement of the display?
Is there a specialist room in each section of the school?
Does each teacher and each set have the chance to use it?
Who is responsible for the displays in it?
Are the display cases used to the maximum?
Do they regularly contain items on loan
— from parents?
— from museums?
— from the record office?
Is a corner of the notice board used to advertise 'forthcoming events'?
Is there a section for History Society notices?
Is there an 'excellent board' for outstanding work?
Is there provision for using audio and visual aids?
— for making models?
— drama?
— group work?
Can half finished models/paintings be stored without creating chaos?
How are slides/film strips/tapes/large maps/posters stored?

Are reference books and readers freely available to pupils at all times?
Is there a good dictionary in the room?
Is there a small staff library?
Is there a catalogue or index of materials available
— for pupils?
— for staff?
Are there cross-references to materials in libraries and other departments?
Has the teacher access to spare notebooks, paper, tracing paper, crayons, etc?
Have the staff access to the room in the evenings, at weekends, holidays?
Is the room used for organised historical activities at lunchtimes, etc.?
Do you play your part in keeping it tidy and free from damage?
Is the room a pleasure to use?

6 *The head of department*

How much interest does the head of department show in each age/ability group?
Does he or she try to sample a cross-section in his or her own teaching allocation?
How much interest does he or she show
— in your teaching?
— in your 'professional development'?
— in your future career?
Do you chat to him or her about your problems, hopes, interests?
On what principles does he or she
— allocate the teaching load?
— plan the syllabus?
— buy books and materials?
Are you consulted in this?
Does he or she delegate?
How efficiently does he or she organise the storing, cataloguing and issue of stock?
How positive is his or her leadership of the department?
Does he or she encourage the department to work as a team?
Does he or she provide enough motivation for improvement?
Does he or she provide enough motivation for experiment?
Does he or she inspire the team?
Does he or she challenge them?
Does he or she encourage them?
Does he or she put pressure on when necessary?
Does he or she encourage informal discussion and call formal meetings?
Does he or she encourage you to attend conferences/courses?
Does he or she guide your decisions on options, recommendations, etc.?
Can you go to him or her confidently for help or advice?
Does he or she represent your views
— to other departments?
— to the school authorities?
— to outside bodies?
Does he or she communicate to you
— details of meetings he or she has attended?
— details of discussions on school policy, etc.?
— his or her own ideas on future departmental policy?
Does he or she secure the support for the department of
— the Inspectorate?
— the LEA Advisory Service?
— local colleges/universities?
How does he or she organise the supervision and training of
— students?
— probationers?
Is he or she involved in the advertising, shortlisting and interview proce-

dures for posts in the Department?
Is he or she involved in the writing of references for members of the department?
Does this fill you with confidence?
Would you miss him or her if he or she left?

7 *Departmental meetings*
Are there regular formal departmental meetings?
Is an agenda issued in advance? Are there minutes afterwards?
Do you normally attend the meetings?
Do you regard them as a chore?
Who suggests the topics for discussion?
Are the meetings used for 'professional advancement'?
Do those who have attended courses report on them?
Do you discuss departmental
— policies?
— aims?
— syllabus?
— examinations?
Do outside speakers ever attend them?
Is the head represented at them?
Do you discuss problems?
Do you play an active part in the discussions?
Do you ever volunteer to prepare and lead a discussion?
Are the decisions translated into action?
Do you share out the administration of the department?
Do you share out the preparation and making of teaching materials?

8 *Out of school activities*
Is there a History Society
— for the older pupils?
— for the pupils in the middle years?
— for the younger pupils?
How many teachers help to run it?
Do the pupils participate in the planning and running of their own society?
Do the older pupils help run the junior societies?
How often does each society meet?
What form do the activities take?
Is it well supported
— by pupils?
— by history teachers?
— by others?
Do you invite outside speakers?
Is there regular contact with similar groups in other schools?
Do you have inter-school quizzes or social activities?
Are visits arranged
— to museums?
— to places of historical interest?
— to lectures to adult societies?
— to exhibitions?
Do the activities ever extend over a weekend?
Has the Society ever arranged or participated in longer activities
— courses?
— tours?
— archaeological digs?
— holidays?
Has it ever arranged foreign visits?
Are the activities reported in the school
— by notices?
— by newsletters?

– in the school magazine?
Are its activities reported in the local press?
Does it publish any research?
Does it ever serve the community beyond the school
– by recording sites?
– by writing guides/trails?
– by exhibitions?
– by acting as hosts/guides?
– in other ways?
Do parents or other outside adults participate in its activities?
If it ceased to exist, would it be missed?

9 *Parents*
How conscientiously do you complete termly reports on pupils?
Are you willing to write special reports on individuals?
How thoroughly do you prepare for parents' evenings?
Are you willing to meet parents by appointment at other times?
Does your department ever use parents' evenings for the following purposes?
– to give illustrated reports on pupils' activities in and out of class?
– explain its aims, problems and policies?
– to demonstrate new teaching techniques?
What is the department's attitude to Open Days?
Do you put on exhibitions
– of pupils' normal work?
– of special projects?
– of a general or local historical interest?
Are parents welcomed into the classroom on certain days?
Are parents regularly encouraged
– to help with classroom group work?
– to help with research homework?
– to help with projects?
– to help with history societies?
– to help supervise fieldwork?
– to participate in excursions?
– to provide transport?
Is there a regularly revised departmental entry in the school prospectus?
– at the first year stage?
– at every option stage?
– at sixth form level?

10 *How well does the department fit into the work and philosophy of the school?*
Does each teacher and pupil understand how history fits into the curriculum?
Do the history teachers regard members of other departments as partners in a climbing team rather than as competitors in a race?
Does the department pursue some at least of the general aims of the school?
Does it exchange experiences with other departments?
Are teaching resources shared with other departments?
Do you attempt to understand and sympathise with their aims and problems?
Do you ever get the opportunity to explain your aims and problems to them?
Are you ever given the opportunity to brief form tutors on the implications for history of the option scheme?
What part does the department play in discussing or deciding the following?
– general matters of school policy?
– the pattern of options?

- the appointment of teachers?
- the allocation of teachers between departments?
- the overall curriculum?
- the timetable?
- the allocation of money?

Is the department always consulted about pupils' choices
- in history?
- in related subjects?

Is the department consulted about careers and references for pupils?

What part does the department play in the in-service training of the school?

Do the head, deputy heads and heads of school understand the department's aims, priorities and problems?

Are they sympathetic?

FURTHER READING

Ballard, M. (ed.), 1970, *New Movements in the Study and Teaching of History*, Temple Smith.
Barker, B., 1977, 'History Situations', in *Teaching History*, no. 17.
Birt, D. and Nichol, J., 1975, *Games and Simulations in History*, Longman.
Blyth, A. et al., 1976, *Place, Time and Society 8-13: Curriculum Planning in History, Geography and Social Science*, Collins.
Blyth, J.E., 1982, *History in Primary Schools*, McGraw Hill.
Bruner, J.S., 1960, *The Process of Education*, Knopf Vintage Books.
Bruner, J.S., 1966, *Towards a Theory of Instruction*, Belknap/Harvard.
Collingwood, R.G., 1946, *The Idea of History*, OUP.
Collingwood, R.G., 1981, 'The teacher's talk' in C.R. Sutton (ed.), *Communicating in the Classroom*, Hodder and Stoughton.
Coltham, J.B. and Fines, J., 1971, *Educational Objectives for the Study of History*, Historical Association, TH35.
Dancy, J. (ed.), 1980, *Perspectives 1 – The Rutter Research*, School of Education, University of Exeter.
Dickinson, A.K. and Lee, P.J. (eds), 1978, *History Teaching and Historical Understanding*, Heinemann.
Fines, J. and Verrier, R., 1974, *The Drama of History*, New University Education.
Hallam, R.N., 'Piaget and thinking in history', see in Ballard, M. (ed.).
Hilsum, S. and Crane, B.S., 1973, *The Teacher's Day*, NFER.
Hilsum, S. and Strong, C., 1978, *The Secondary Teacher's Day*, National Foundation for Educational Research.
Jones, J.A.P., 1978, *History in the Making Series*, Macmillan.
Kerry, T. and Bell, P., 1982, *Teaching Slow Learners*, Macmillan, *Focus* books.
Kerry, T. and Sands, M.K., 1982, *Handling Classroom Groups*, Macmillan, *Focus* books.
Kerry, T. (ed.), 1983, *Finding and Helping the Able Child*, Croom Helm.
Lawton, D. and Dufour, B., 1973, *The New Social Studies*, Heinemann.
Lawton, D. (ed.), 1978, *Theory and Practice of Curriculum Studies*, Routledge and Kegan Paul.
Levine, N., 1981, *Language Teaching and Learning – History*, Ward Lock.
Macintosh, H.G., 1976, *Assessment and the Secondary School Teacher*, Routledge and Kegan Paul.
Marland, M. (ed.), 1977, *Language Across the Curriculum*, Heinemann.
Martin, N. et al., 1976, *Writing and Learning Across the Curriculum*, Schools Council.
Marwick, A., 1970, *The Meaning of History*, Macmillan.
Nichol, J. (ed.), 1980, *Perspectives 4 – Developments in History Teaching*, School of Education, University of Exeter.

Palmer, M. and Batho, G.R., 1981, *The Source Method in History Teaching,* Historical Association, TH48.

Rogers, P.J., *The New History: theory into practice*, Historical Association, TH44.

Rutter, M. et al., 1979, *Fifteen Thousand Hours,* Open Books.

Schools Council, 1976, *Schools Council Project History 13-16,* Holmes McDougall.

Shemilt, D.J., 1980, 'Schools Council Project "History 13-16": Past, Present and Future' in *History Teaching Review*, vol. 12.1.

Steel, D. and Taylor, L., 1973, *Family History in Schools,* Phillimore.

Steele, I., 1976, *Developments in History Teaching*, Open Books.

Sutton, C.R. (ed.), 1981, *Communicating in the Classroom,* Hodder and Stoughton.

Teaching History, no. 17, Feb. 1977; no. 21, June 1978; no. 28, Oct. 1978; No. 33, June 1982; No. 34, Oct. 1982.

Unwin, R., 1981, *The Visual Dimension in the Study and Teaching of History,* Historical Association, TH49.

Warwick, D. (ed.), 1973, *Integrated Studies in the Secondary School,* Hodder and Stoughton.

Wragg, E.C., 1981, *Class Management and Control,* Macmillan, *Focus* books.